McGRAW-HILL'S

Pocket Guide to Spirometry

Second edition

David P. Johns
PhD, CRFS, FANZSRS
Principal Research Fellow, Menzies Research Institute,
University of Tasmania

Rob Pierce
MBBS, MD, FRACP, FCCP
Professor/Director of Respiratory and Sleep Medicine,
University of Melbourne and Austin Hospital

The McGraw·Hill Companies

Sydney New York San Francisco Auckland
Bangkok Bogotá Caracas Hong Kong
Kuala Lumpur Lisbon London Madrid
Mexico City Milan New Delhi San Juan
Seoul Singapore Taipei Toronto

Professional

Text © 2007 Rob Pierce and David Johns
Illustrations and design © 2007 McGraw-Hill Australia Pty Ltd. Reprinted 2009
Additional owners of copyright are acknowledged on the Acknowledgments page.

National Library of Australia Cataloguing-in-Publication data:
Johns, David Peter, 1952- .
McGraw-Hill's pocket guide to spirometry.

2nd ed.
Includes index.
ISBN 9780070134645.

1. Spirometry. 2. Pulmonary function tests.
I. Pierce, Rob, 1947– . II. Title

616.24075

Published in Australia by
McGraw-Hill Australia Pty Ltd
Level 2, 82 Waterloo Road, North Ryde NSW 2113
Publisher: Nicole Meehan
Production Editor: Leanne Poll
Editor: Leanne Poll
Proofreader: Tess Hardman
Indexer: Glenda Browne
Design (cover and interior): Lara Scott, Unhinged Productions
Illustrator: Anne McLean, Jobs On Mac
Typeset in 9.5 pt Sabon by Anne McLean, Jobs On Mac
Printed on 80 gsm Wood Free in China by 1010 Printing International Limited

The McGraw·Hill Companies

Foreword to the first edition

Spirometry is spirometry is spirometry. It matters not if this measurement of lung function is performed in an accredited lung function laboratory at a major hospital, by an occupational health nurse at a remote mining site or by a general physician at his/her practice. The same general principles must apply to all in order to achieve an accurate result. Unfortunately this is not always the case. There is a perception that by simply combining a patient with a spirometer, accurate results of high quality are automatically produced, with apparently little thought afforded to the accuracy of the device performing the measurement, the effort of the subject undertaking the test or the competence of the person supervising the test. Despite the ready availability of internationally accepted guidelines for the performance of spirometry, the literature abounds with reports of spirometry measurements of such poor quality to render it useless at best, to downright dangerous should this result be incorrectly interpreted.

It is now recognised that only a good understanding of lung physiology plus appropriate education in all aspects of spirometry can overcome the problems associated with this measurement. Careful reading of this book will certainly provide readers with a thorough understanding of spirometry from calibration through to interpretation.

This excellent publication, and indeed its precursor—*Spirometry: The Measurement and Interpretation of Ventilatory Function in Clinical Practice*—represents another chapter in the ongoing commitment of David and Rob to raise the standard of spirometry performed in Australia and New Zealand. In this publication, David and Rob have added sections that will be particularly useful at the 'coalface' (e.g. spirometry in children, the FEV_6 and case histories). They have also taken the extra step of including a section on the mechanics of breathing which succinctly demonstrates how normal (and abnormal) physiology can affect measurements of spirometry and greatly assist in its interpretation.

We have no doubt this publication will shortly become the popular spirometry reference book in Australia and New Zealand and strongly endorse its use by all healthcare professionals performing spirometry and indeed all measurements of ventilatory function.

Brenton Eckert, President, Australian & New Zealand Society of Respiratory Science

Richard Ruffin, President, Thoracic Society of Australia and New Zealand.

March 2003

Foreword to the second edition

The second edition of the *Pocket Guide to Spirometry* by David Johns and Rob Pierce is likely to be even more popular than the first as the changes that have been incorporated enhance and update this excellent resource. Additions include incorporation throughout of the 2005 American Thoracic Society and European Respiratory Society joint recommendations on spirometry measurement and interpretation, as well as a change to the more recent and robust reference equations for normal spirometry of Hankinson, Odencrantz and Fedan (1999). Importantly, the succinct and conversational style that has made the book accessible to the full range of health professional readers and the vital sections explaining the underlying physiology of the mechanics of breathing, vital to understanding what is being measured by spirometry, are retained.

This book is useful for all with an interest in optimal measurement and interpretation of spirometry, whether they are novices or are using it as a resource as they acquire further experience. A primary aim of the Australian and New Zealand Society of Respiratory Science is to support and encourage education and training in respiratory science and excellence in respiratory measurement, and it is for this reason that we proudly endorse this excellent publication.

Debbie Burton, New South Wales Representative/Board member, Australian & New Zealand Society of Respiratory Science

Graham Hall, President, Australian & New Zealand Society of Respiratory Science

March 2007

Contents

Preface

This second edition of *Pocket Guide to Spirometry* has been updated throughout to comply with the latest spirometry standards developed jointly by the American Thoracic Society and the European Respiratory Society. Predicted normal value tables have been completely revised to NHANES III and extended to include indices based on a 6-second expiration and lower limit of normal for all indices. A number of changes have been made in response to suggestions by readers for which we are very grateful.

Over recent years there has been a growing recognition of the value of spirometry in clinical medicine and physicians are now being encouraged to include the measurement in their clinical practice. However, it is often not appreciated that clinically useful results are critically dependent on the accuracy of the spirometer and the competence of the operator in instructing and motivating the patient to perform the correct breathing manoeuvre.

The main reason for writing this book was to help improve the quality of spirometry measurements and their interpretation, and to encourage the use of spirometry in clinical medicine. We have attempted to provide a practical guide for those involved in the performance and interpretation of spirometry—medical practitioners and assisting nursing staff, respiratory scientists, technologists, technicians, physiotherapists and other healthcare workers.

This book is not intended to be an exhaustive review but rather a guide to help improve the knowledge and techniques of those already doing and interpreting spirometry, and to introduce spirometry to those learning how to do it for the first time. The important facts about the physiology of normal airflow and the pathophysiology underlying spirometric deficits are given, as is practical information about types of spirometers and how the test is actually performed and interpreted. Some common pitfalls and problems are covered in the main text. Case histories taken from clinical practice are used to illustrate the diagnostic value of airflow and lung volume measurement.

Acknowledgments

We are most grateful to the National Asthma Council who in 1995 published our original handbook on which this book is based (*Spirometry: The Measurement and Interpretation of Ventilatory Function in Clinical Practice*). We are also indebted to two outstanding teachers of respiratory physiology, Dr Alistair Campbell and Dr David Denison. We wish to thank the many colleagues who offered advice and support, especially Professor E. Haydn Walters, Brenton Eckert, Kevin Gain, Debbie Burton, Maureen Swanney, Andrew Coates, Eleonora Side, Sandra Anderson and Peter Rochford. There are also a number of professional organisations to whom we are most grateful for providing valuable advice which has helped maintain the relevance of this book as a practical guide: Australian and New Zealand Society of Respiratory Science, Thoracic Society of Australia and New Zealand and Royal College of General Practitioners. Finally, Lesley Pocock, Director of Mediworld Inc., has been extremely helpful in providing professional advice and for the publication of our interactive multimedia CD-ROM on spirometry (*Spirometry*), which includes an abridged electronic version of this book.

About the authors

David Johns

Associate Professor David Johns is a respiratory physiologist with a particular interest in research and undergraduate and postgraduate teaching. He is currently Principal Research Fellow, Menzies Research Institute, University of Tasmania, Hobart, Tasmania. He commenced his respiratory career in 1972 at the Brompton Heart and Chest Hospital, United Kingdom, and moved to Australia in 1978 where for the next 23 years he developed and managed respiratory laboratories at Victoria's Austin and Alfred Hospitals.

His research interests are focused on the physiological consequences of airway modelling, mathematical modelling of gas exchange and lung function testing. He is actively engaged with the medical profession, national professional organisations, government and industry. He is currently on the board of the Australian and New Zealand Society of Respiratory Science (ANZSRS), media spokesperson on lung function for the National Asthma Council of Australia and member of a number of scientific committees.

David has published original research papers, textbooks, online books, book chapters and interactive multimedia CD-ROMs. His contributions to respiratory research were recognised in 2002 when he was awarded the ANZSRS Research Medal (Fellowship).

Rob Pierce

Rob Pierce is Professor/Director of Respiratory and Sleep Medicine at the University of Melbourne and the Austin Hospital in Heidelberg, Victoria. He is also a foundation Medical Director of the Institute for Breathing and Sleep (at the Austin), which promotes research, education and public advocacy in respiratory and sleep health. He has been associated with the respiratory laboratory at the Austin Hospital since the early 1980s and has led the working group on guidelines for lung function testing for the Thoracic Society of Australia and New Zealand.

His MD thesis was concerned with measurement of lung and lobar volumes and the accuracy of various measurement techniques and was completed at the Brompton Hospital in the United Kingdom. He has published extensively in peer-reviewed scientific journals and co-authored with David Johns the interactive CD-ROM, *Spirometry*.

Rob has taught respiratory physiology and medicine at University of Melbourne for many years. His clinical research interests include the physiology, function and disease of both lower and upper airways. He was recently a foundation investigator in the Australasian Sleep Trials Network which, among other clinical areas, supports research into the impact of sleep on airway physiology and the clinical consequences of sleep-disordered breathing.

Introduction

A great deal can be learned about the mechanical properties of the lungs from measurements of maximal expiration and inspiration. Since Hutchinson first developed the spirometer in 1846, measurements of the so-called dynamic lung volumes and of maximal flows have been used in the detection and quantification of diseases affecting the respiratory system. Over the years it has become obvious that the spirometer and peak flow meter used to measure ventilatory function are as deserving of a place in the family practitioner's surgery as the sphygmomanometer. After all, who would dream of managing hypertension without measurement of blood pressure?

Respiratory disease is a major clinical problem. At the date of publication of this book, about one in four children and one in five adults in some countries, including Australia and New Zealand, have asthma and there is evidence that the prevalence is increasing. In Australia alone over 2.2 million people have a diagnosis of asthma and it is estimated that the health costs associated with the care of people with asthma is as high as $720 000 000 per year. In addition, 10% to 20% of adults over 17 years of age have chronic obstructive pulmonary disease (COPD) with the odds ratio for developing COPD increasing dramatically with smoking and age. Despite these disturbing statistics only 25% to 33% of those with measurable airflow obstruction in general practice have a diagnosis or are aware of their respiratory problem. Also, in the United Kingdom (UK) only 50% of doctors in general practice have access to spirometry in their practice (39% in 1996). By the year 2020, COPD will be the third most common overall cause of death, representing 11% of deaths from any cause. In these diseases, spirometry is essential for the diagnosis and the assessment of response to therapy.

There are now simple, accurate, robust and reliable spirometers that enable ventilatory function to be measured in a doctor's surgery as readily as in a hospital respiratory function laboratory. There are also portable devices that enable patients with lung disease to monitor their own progress and the status of their lung disease. The self-monitoring of peak flow by people with asthma and its use to regulate their treatment with anti-inflammatory and bronchodilator drugs is a natural extension of the ease with which ventilatory function can now be monitored reliably.

The role of spirometry in case finding in general practice and in screening of high-risk populations has recently begun to be evaluated in relation to the high prevalence and vast under-diagnosis of respiratory disease in the general population and the even greater prevalence in high-risk populations, for example smokers over 40 years of age and in certain occupational settings.

It is important to appreciate that the clinical value of spirometric measurements is critically dependent on the correct operation and accuracy of the spirometer, performance of the correct breathing manoeuvre, selection of the best results and use of relevant predicted normal values.

It is very clear, therefore, that spirometry should be readily available in general practice and the measurement of ventilatory capacity should be regarded as mandatory for many patients.

Spirometry training

It is important that staff performing spirometry first attend a comprehensive training course. This is because inadequate training will result in poor quality spirometry which is of little clinical value. As a minimum these courses should provide adequate training in how to:
- maintain and validate the spirometer
- perform the correct breathing manoeuvre
- identify and overcome poor technique
- select and report the results of spirometry.

Lists of endorsed spirometry training courses in Australia and New Zealand are available on the websites of the

Australian and New Zealand Society of Respiratory Science (www.anzsrs.org.au) and the Thoracic Society of Australia and New Zealand (www.thoracic.org.au).

> *[Spirometry] should be readily available and routinely used in medical offices and hospitals where patients with heart and lung diseases are treated.*
>
> (Dr Robert O. Crapo, 'Pulmonary function testing', *New England Journal of Medicine*, 1994, 331(1), pp. 25–30)

PART 1

Chapter 1

What is spirometry and what are its uses?

Spirometry is a physiological test of lung function, so in order to introduce it a brief summary of the function of the pulmonary system is appropriate.

The function of the lung and lung function tests

The primary function of the lungs is to arterialise mixed venous blood to meet the metabolic demands of the body (Figure 1.1). If the lungs are functioning normally, they will produce arterialised blood of normal composition and they will do this even during strenuous exercise. The lung achieves this by bringing almost the entire output from the heart into intimate contact with the air we breathe. If lung function is normal, at sea level arterial blood will have a P_{CO_2} of about 40 mmHg and a P_{O_2} close to 100 mmHg.

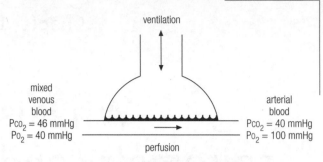

The lungs arterialise venous blood

Figure 1.1 Simplified model of the lung showing ventilation and blood flow. The average normal adult lung has a total lung capacity of about 6.5 litres, about 300 million alveoli and is almost continuously perfused by a flow of blood equal to the cardiac output. At rest we breathe 5–10 L/min and cardiac output is about 5 L/min. The blood perfusing the alveoli is so thinly spread that at any instant the volume participating in gas exchange is only about 80 mL.

There are several component processes that interact to determine the effectiveness of lung function to meet the metabolic demands of the body's tissues:
- *ventilation*: capacity of the respiratory system to move air into and out of all the gas-exchanging regions of the lung containing pulmonary capillary blood
- *pulmonary blood flow*: capacity of the circulatory system to deliver mixed venous blood to all the gas-exchanging regions of the lung
- *diffusion*: passive movement of CO_2 and O_2 across the alveolar–capillary membrane that separates air in the alveoli from blood perfusing the pulmonary capillaries. The process of gas diffusion and pulmonary blood flow are collectively described as the gas-exchange function of the lungs.
- *control of ventilation*: regulation of ventilation to ensure adequate arterialisation of mixed venous blood to meet metabolic demands.

Each of these components interacts with the others, and all are essential for normal lung function. There is no single test of lung function that will assess all of the above components of lung function, but many tests, each of which will assess one or more of the various components of function. Spirometry is the measurement of respired or dynamic lung volumes. Other tests, for example respiratory muscle strength and airway reactivity, assess other aspects of ventilation. Diffusing capacity (or transfer factor) and arterial blood gas tensions, used in conjunction with the alveolar gas equation, are used to assess gas exchange and the integrity of the alveolar–capillary membrane. Exercise tests are used to evaluate integrated pulmonary and cardio-pulmonary function under conditions of increased metabolic demand.

The single most broadly useful non-invasive test of ventilatory lung function is spirometry. This is because impaired ventilatory function is the most common physiological abnormality affecting the lung (for example, asthma and COPD). The most common cause of impaired ventilatory function is airway narrowing. This may be due to loss of traction from the surrounding lung tissue as in emphysema, to inflammation of the walls of the airway, mucus plugging and bronchospasm as in asthma, or to obstruction of the airway lumen caused, for instance, by a tumour. Other causes of impaired ventilatory function include respiratory muscle weakness or paralysis, cardiac enlarge-ment, or alterations to the lung, chest wall or pleura that limit the full expansion or the rate of emptying of the lung.

Spirometry is therefore an important test to detect, quantify and monitor diseases that limit ventilatory capacity—the mechanical properties of the lung and chest wall that affect the lung's volume and the calibre of the airways.

Indications for spirometry

The following list summarises the wide range of indications for spirometry (see also Miller et al. 2005b):
- detecting and assessing respiratory disease in patients presenting with symptoms of breathlessness either at rest

or on exertion, wheeze, cough, stridor, phlegm production, etc.

- assessing respiratory function in all smokers and people exposed to polluted environments and in those with a family history of respiratory disease
- differentiating respiratory from cardiac disease as the cause of breathlessness
- screening for respiratory disease in certain high-risk situations and populations, for example smokers (especially over 40 years of age), pre-employment in industries in which occupational asthma is prevalent, and identifying those at risk from activities such as scuba diving
- diagnosing respiratory disease, differentiating obstructive versus restrictive ventilatory defects and identifying upper airway obstruction and diseases associated with weakness of the respiratory muscles
- assessing the severity and following the natural history and progression of respiratory and sometimes systemic and neuromuscular diseases
- assessing response to treatment
- assessing impairment from respiratory disease in the workplace and in the settings of pulmonary rehabilitation and compensation for occupational lung disease
- assessing preoperative risk prior to anaesthesia and abdominal or thoracic surgery.

Complications and contraindications

Spirometry is generally a safe, non-invasive procedure. However, it does require maximal effort and subject cooperation, which may result in transient breathlessness, oxygen desaturation, syncope, chest pain and cough. The forced manoeuvre can also induce bronchospasm in patients with poorly controlled asthma. There are a number of clinical circumstances in which the generation of a high positive intra-thoracic pressure and its transmission to vascular, abdominal and other body compartments may be detrimental and thus spirometry is best avoided. The measurement of spirometry is thus normally delayed following:

- recent eye surgery
- recent thoracic and abdominal surgery
- aneurysms (for example cerebral, abdominal)
- unstable cardiac function
- haemoptysis of unknown cause
- pneumothorax
- chest and abdominal pain
- nausea and diarrhoea.

Summary

Spirometry is a very useful non-invasive test to detect, quantify and monitor diseases that limit ventilatory function. The test is relatively easy to perform although it does require maximal effort, and patient cooperation is essential. Spirometry is generally a safe test, although it can induce bronchospasm in patients with poorly controlled asthma and there are several contraindications where it is unwise to proceed with the test.

Chapter 2

Measurement of ventilatory function

C onventionally, a spirometer is a device used to measure timed expired and inspired volumes, and from these we can calculate how effectively and how quickly the lungs can be emptied and filled. Spirometry is usually recorded as either a *spirogram* (a plot of volume versus time) or *flow-volume curve* or *loop* (a plot of volume versus flow).

The spirogram

Figure 2.1 shows two commonly recorded spirograms. The measurements that are usually made are as follows:

- **FVC** (forced vital capacity) and **VC** (vital capacity) are the maximum volume of air that can be expired or inspired during either a forced (FVC) or a slow (VC) manoeuvre. The FVC is normally equal to the VC unless airway closure occurs during the forced expiratory manoeuvre, in which case the VC is higher than FVC. The difference between VC and FVC is often referred to as 'trapped gas'.
- **FEV_1** (forced expired volume in 1 second) is the volume expired in the first second of maximal expiration (initiated after a maximal inspiration) and is a very widely used measure of how quickly full lungs can be emptied.

- **FEV$_1$/VC ratio** (or FEV$_1$/FVC) is the FEV$_1$ expressed as a percentage of the VC or FVC (whichever volume is larger) and gives a clinically useful index of airflow limitation. It is essentially the proportion of the lung volume that can be expired in 1 second and is also referred to as the forced expiratory ratio, FER%.
- **FEF$_{25-75\%}$** or **MEF$_{25-75\%}$** (forced or maximal expiratory flow over the middle half of the FVC manoeuvre) is the average expired flow over the middle half of the FVC manoeuvre and is regarded as a more sensitive measure of peripheral or small airways narrowing than FEV$_1$. Unfortunately FEF$_{25-75\%}$ has a wide range of normality, is less reproducible than FEV$_1$ and is difficult to interpret if the FVC is reduced or increased. (This index was formerly termed the maximal mid-expiratory flow rate, MMEFR.)
- **FET** (forced expiratory time) is the time required to perform the FVC manoeuvre (usually less than 5–6 seconds in adults and 2–3 seconds in children). The FET is increased in the presence of airflow limitation (often > 12 seconds).

Indices based on 6-second forced expiration

Spirometric indices calculated using a 6-second volume base instead of the vital capacity are gaining popularity (Ferguson et al. 2000). Stopping the expiratory manoeuvre after 6 seconds has the advantage of decreasing the physical demands of performing spirometry and potentially reducing their coefficient of variation. This is an advantage for patients with significant airway obstruction as well as the elderly and physically impaired. Also, the variations in forced vital capacity due to variations in expiratory time are eliminated if we substitute FVC$_6$ for FVC. The diagnostic criteria are equivalent to the traditional FVC-based parameters. Many portable spirometers now have these 6-second parameters available in their software:

- **FVC$_6$**—largest forced expiratory volume measured during the first 6 seconds. This is similar to FEV$_6$ which is the forced expiratory volume measure *at* 6 seconds.

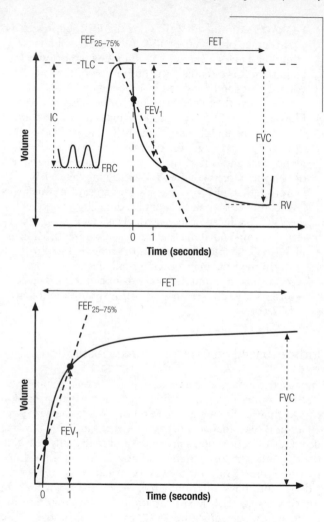

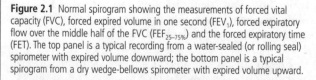

Figure 2.1 Normal spirogram showing the measurements of forced vital capacity (FVC), forced expired volume in one second (FEV$_1$), forced expiratory flow over the middle half of the FVC (FEF$_{25-75\%}$) and the forced expiratory time (FET). The top panel is a typical recording from a water-sealed (or rolling seal) spirometer with expired volume downward; the bottom panel is a typical spirogram from a dry wedge-bellows spirometer with expired volume upward.

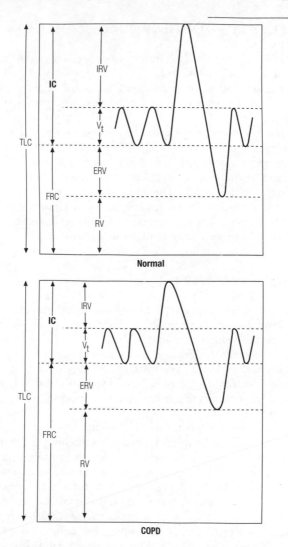

Figure 2.2 The lung volumes and capacities in normal and hyperinflated lungs (for example, COPD). The inspiratory capacity (IC) is the volume that can be inspired from FRC. TLC = total lung capacity; RV = residual volume; FRC = functional residual capacity; IC = inspiratory capacity; ERV = expiratory reserve volume; IRV = inspiratory reserve volume; V_t = tidal volume.

- **FEV_1/FVC_6**—FEV_1 expressed as a percentage of the FVC_6
- **$FEF_{25-75\%6}$**—forced expiratory flow over the middle half of the FVC_6 manoeuvre.

It is important to use appropriate reference values (that is, based on a 6-second expiration) when interpreting these indices.

Studies have reported that these parameters are equivalent to the traditional FVC and FEV_1/FVC for the diagnosis of obstructive and restrictive patterns and for predicting decline in smokers (Swanney et al. 2000; Enright et al. 2002). The clinical utility of $FEF_{25-75\%}$ is limited because of the large variation in this index, which is partly due to its dependence on FVC. However, using FVC_6 as the volume base may reduce this variation.

Inspiratory capacity

The inspiratory capacity, IC, is the maximum volume of air that can be inspired from the end of quiet expiration (from functional residual capacity, FRC, to total lung capacity, TLC)—see Figure 2.2. This index is gaining popularity as a measure of dynamic hyperinflation during exercise and as a measure of the degree of reduced hyperinflation following the administration of a bronchodilator, especially in COPD (see p. 62).

This measurement of IC using an open-circuit spirometry (see Chapter 4) involves switching the patient into this circuit at the end of quiet expiration (that is, functional residual capacity) and measuring the maximum volume that can be inspired (that is, to total lung capacity).

Closed-circuit spirometry facilitates the measurement of IC by affording the operator the capacity to scrutinise the stability of FRC during tidal breathing before asking the patient to inspire fully. Volume-displacement spirometers must contain a volume of air at the start of the manoeuvre that is greater than the patient's inspiratory capacity so that a full inspiratory breath can be measured.

Flow spirometers, provided they have the software to integrate inspiratory as well as expiratory flow, are usually more suitable as they do not require the patient to breathe in from an air reservoir.

The flow-volume curve or loop

Measures of maximum flow can be made either absolutely (for example, peak expiratory flow) or expressed as a function of volume, the latter by generating a flow-volume curve (expiration only) or flow-volume loop (expiration followed by inspiration—Figure 2.3). The shape of this curve is reproducible for any individual but varies considerably between different lung diseases. A poorly performed manoeuvre is usually characterised by alterations in the shape of the curve and by poor

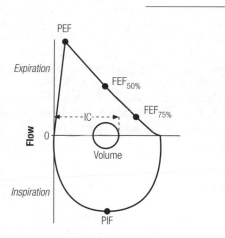

Figure 2.3 Normal maximal flow-volume loop showing the peak expiratory and inspiratory flows (PEF and PIF) and maximum flows after 50% and 75% of the FVC had been expired ($FEF_{50\%}$ and $FEF_{75\%}$). Note that in health the shape of the flow-volume curve is a straight-sided triangle (expiration) on top of a deep semicircle (inspiration). Respiratory disease can dramatically alter the shape of the flow-volume loop.

reproducibility. The measurements derived from the flow-volume curve include those above, and:

- $FEF_{50\%}$ and $FEF_{75\%}$ (forced expiratory flow at 50% or 75% FVC), which are the maximal expiratory flow measured at the point where 50% of the FVC has been expired ($FEF_{50\%}$) and after 75% has been expired ($FEF_{75\%}$). Both indices have a wide range of normality but are usually reproducible in a given subject, provided the FVC is reproducible.
- PEF (peak expiratory flow), which is the maximal expiratory flow achieved. This occurs very early in the forced expiratory manoeuvre. The PEF is an index of airflow limitation mainly due to obstruction in the large airways.
- PIF (peak inspiratory flow), which is the maximal inspiratory flow achieved. Unlike the PEF, the PIF occurs at about 50% FVC.

All indices of ventilatory function (volumes and flows) should be reported at body temperature and pressure saturated with water vapour (BTPS) (Miller et al. 2005b). If this is not done the results will be underestimated because when the patient blows into a 'cold' spirometer, the volume recorded by the spirometer is less than that displaced by the lungs. The expired gas cools to a degree dependent on the temperature inside the spirometer—normally the ambient temperature of the room (see Appendix B).

Summary

Spirometry is usually recorded as either a spirogram or a flow-volume curve (or loop). The most commonly measured indices are FEV_1, FVC, FEV_1/FVC ratio, PEF and $FEF_{25-75\%}$. Also, indices based on the 6-second forced expiration (FVC_6) and the inspiratory capacity (as a measure of dynamic hyperinflation) are gaining popularity. The shape of the flow-volume curve often provides very useful additional and complementary information. All measurements of volume and flow are reported after correction to BTPS conditions.

Chapter 3

Measurement devices

Spirometers can be categorised as either volume-displacement or flow spirometers depending on whether they primarily measure volume or flow (Figure 3.1). Flow spirometers are the most commonly used and are available as full diagnostic instruments or monitors with limited functionality. The minimum performance standards for all spirometers are summarised in Appendix A (Table A.1).

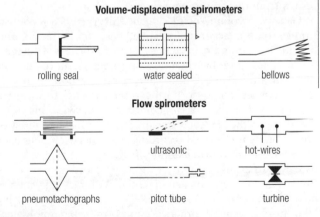

Volume-displacement spirometers

rolling seal   water sealed   bellows

Flow spirometers

ultrasonic   hot-wires

pneumotachographs   pitot tube   turbine

Figure 3.1 Schematic diagrams showing examples of volume-displacement and flow spirometers in common use

Volume-displacement spirometers

These are conventional spirometers that provide a direct measure of respired volume from the displacement of a bell (water-sealed), piston (rolling seal) or bellows (for example, wedge bellows).

The results are normally presented as a graphic display of expired volume against time (a spirogram). The indices FEV_1, FVC and VC are generally manually calculated (including back-extrapolation—see Chapter 4—and correction to BTPS—see Appendix B) from the spirogram by the operator and for this reason volume-displacement spirometers are sometimes considered time-consuming and less convenient for routine use in a busy doctor's surgery. $FEF_{25-75\%}$ is also sometimes measured as an index of early disease affecting the peripheral airways (for example, in asymptomatic smokers). Some volume-displacement spirometers are computer-assisted to reduce testing time as all computations, including correction to BTPS, are performed automatically. An important advantage of computerised volume-displacement spirometers which also incorporate a kymograph (rotating drum to move the recording paper) is that the operator can manually verify the accuracy of the computer-derived results from the simultaneously recorded spirogram.

Generally, volume-displacement spirometers are robust, simple to use, accurate, reliable, easy to maintain and provide a clear and permanent record of the test. They are, however, less portable than flow spirometers, more difficult to clean and disinfect and have relatively poor dynamic characteristics. Some do not have the capacity to measure inspiratory volumes or to compare tidal with maximal breathing. Although their dynamic response characteristics are adequate for faithful recording of events occurring over a second or more (for example FVC, FEV_1), they are not usually sufficiently fast to accurately record rapid events (for example, PEF measurements). Volume spirometers have been and are still widely used in respiratory laboratories, general practice clinics and epidemiological surveys of lung function and are the instruments most familiar to clinicians. However, spirometers utilising flow sensors are now more popular and have advantages in terms of portability, infection control and, in many, the capacity to measure inspiratory volumes (for example IC, IVC, FIV_1), and to compare tidal breathing with the flow-volume loop.

Flow spirometers

Over recent years, advances in electronics and low-cost microprocessor technology have led to the development of a wide range of flow spirometers. Flow spirometers utilise a sensor that measures flow as the primary signal and calculates volume by electronic (analogue) or numerical (digital) integration of the flow signal. The most commonly used flow sensors detect and measure flow from the pressure drop across a known, constant resistance (for example, pneumotachograph or orifice); cooling of one or more heated wires (anemometer); transmission of ultrasonic sound waves; or by electronically counting the rotation of a turbine blade.

For the family practitioner, these devices have largely replaced the manual volume-displacement spirometer. This is because they are usually easily portable, automatically calculate all ventilatory indices, correct values to BTPS conditions, provide immediate feedback on the acceptability of each test attempted, select the best results, store patient results, calculate normal reference values and lower limit of normal for the patient being tested and provide a print-out of the results including the spirogram and flow-volume curve. Some also provide an interpretation of the results, but the appropriateness of these comments depends on the use of correct predicted normal values and rules employed by the software to classify ventilatory defects and grade their severity.

These features, together with their lower price, ease of use and maintenance (for example, cleaning and disinfection) have made flow-based spirometers very popular. Their capacity to measure inspiratory volumes is another major advantage.

Some flow spirometers have single patient use disposable sensors which also serve as the mouthpiece, effectively eliminating the need for cleaning and disinfection. However, the accuracy of each new sensor needs to be established. Accuracy and reproducibility depend on the stability and calibration of the electronic circuitry and appropriate correction of flow and volume to BTPS conditions (see Appendix B). For example, a small error when detecting zero flow (that is, drift) may cause some devices to produce large errors in the measurement of FVC, as the error may be continually added during the time needed to complete the blow.

With heavy use, the sensor may also change its calibration due to the condensation of water vapour, deposition of mucus or changes in the mechanical operation of the sensor. Even the presence of the finest hair can interfere with the free rotation of a turbine or the calibration of a hot-wire anemometer. Knowledge and application of regular calibration procedures are required to detect such errors and are an essential part of the care of these machines, as they are of any other spirometer.

Further, not all flow spirometers provide flexibility in the choice of normal reference values relevant to your population or allow the operator to manually enter personally selected, predicted equations.

At present, some spirometers also limit the user's capacity to fully configure the format of the printed report, including the choice of lung function indices, and may lack custom-isation to include the name and address of your business.

Monitoring devices and peak flow meters

Monitoring devices are spirometers which are suitable for frequent, repeated use for serially assessing and quantifying change in ventilatory function. Note that monitoring devices have to meet the same equipment requirements (for example, accuracy) as diagnostic spirometers (Miller et al. 2005b). (See Appendix A.) They are usually less expensive and measure a limited range of indices.

Mechanical devices for personal use by patients, such as the peak flow meter, have been available for several decades for serial monitoring of lung function and have proven useful in the management of asthma. Typically, they use the principle of airflow through a tube causing the displacement of a spring-loaded disc which in turn displaces a marker along a scale calibrated in litres per minute. Most peak flow meters are robust and provide reproducible results essential for serial monitoring. However, they often have limited accuracy and, because they provide only a single effort-dependent index of ventilatory function and do not provide a graphical display to check patient effort, they have limited application in the initial assessment of respiratory diseases.

The PEF is reduced in diseases causing airways obstruction and to a lesser extent in neuromuscular diseases in which there is reduced expiratory muscle strength. Peak flow monitoring is particularly useful for following trends in lung function, quantifying response to treatment and identifying trigger factors in asthma. This is because these devices have high precision and can detect changes in PEF.

Peak flow meters can vary considerably in accuracy between brands; this is sometimes due to the complex physical characteristics of the spring component resulting in non-linear performance. The accuracy of some peak flow meters has been enhanced through the use of a non-linear measurement scale; that is, they are calibrated to compensate for non-linearity in their physical performance.

Also available are peak flow meters which produce a whistle when the patient's PEF achieves a preset level (as set by the patient's physician). These devices are useful for children ('if you can make it whistle, then your lungs are okay'), for the vision-impaired and for quick assessment at night in the dark.

Recently, small, reliable, inexpensive yet accurate, battery-powered electronic devices for measuring ventilatory function (including FEV_1) have been developed. Some can store the test data with date and time, which can be downloaded onto a computer for review and statistical analysis. As mentioned, monitoring devices have to meet the same equipment standards as full-performance spirometers.

These devices are becoming more popular as their price decreases with increasing demand and may eventually replace the traditional peak flow meter.

Calibration and quality control

Accurate and reliable spirometry requires an ongoing program of preventative maintenance that includes regular cleaning and calibration (or validation) checks to ensure that the machine is operating correctly and consistently providing clinically useful results. Most electronic spirometers incorporate a specific calibration subroutine as part of the software whereas volume-displacement spirometers often require the calibration to be done manually. All diagnostic spirometers must be capable of being calibrated or having their calibration checked, and this should be done regularly. Be wary of claims by some manufacturers that their spirometer does not require calibration. However, it is true that some brands of spirometer have been shown to maintain their accuracy over long periods.

3 litre calibration syringe

From a practical point of view, the accuracy of a spirometer is checked using a certified 3.00 litre calibration syringe and the procedure is normally carried out via a calibration subroutine. When the 3 litres is passed into the spirometer it should record a volume to within ±3.5% (Miller et al. 2005b). That is, the spirometer is accurate if the recorded volume is between 2.895 and 3.105 litres ATPS.

Flow spirometers should also be checked weekly for *linearity* over the physiological range of flows (ideally 0–14 L/s). A good test of linearity (and accuracy) is to deliver the 3.00 litres several times at different rates to cover a wide range of flows. If the spirometer is linear, the volume recorded will remain between 2.895 and 3.105 litres over the flow range—see Figure 3.2. Records of calibration checks, quality control and service history should be recorded in a logbook and kept with the

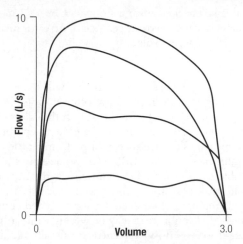

Figure 3.2 Checking the accuracy and linearity of the flow spirometer requires a 3.00 litre syringe to be emptied at several speeds. In this example, the spirometer is accurate over a wide flow range because the volume measured by the spirometer was always between the ERS/ATS accuracy limits of 2.895 and 3.105 litres.

equipment. It is important to remember that, as with any mechanical device, a calibration syringe should be checked for correct performance and accuracy periodically. Leaks can be checked easily but the accuracy of the syringe needs to be checked by the supplier or manufacturer.

Volume-displacement spirometers should be checked for volume linearity every 3 months by consecutive injections of one-litre increments from a calibration syringe (Miller et al. 2005b).

Leaks and timing accuracy
Volume-displacement spirometers should be checked daily for *leaks* by filling the spirometer and applying a weight to the spirometer bell (or by applying a constant pressure ≥ 3 cmH$_2$0 or 0.3 kPa) with breathing hoses attached and plugged, and observing any volume change. In practice, a volume change of less than 0.03 litres over a 60-second period is acceptable. If a kymograph is fitted the *paper speed*

should also be checked with a stopwatch every 3 months or immediately when an error is suspected. An error in accuracy of within 2% is acceptable.

Frequency
The frequency of performing checks will vary with the clinical setting (for example, how often it is used) and the type of spirometer, and the need to adjust the calibration will depend on whether its accuracy is within acceptable limits. Table 3.1 provides the frequency of performing these checks as recommended by the ERS/ATS. Some spirometers are more stable than others. For example, in the absence of a leak, volume-displacement spirometers such as the rolling seal usually maintain their accuracy for extended periods and the frequency of calibration may be weekly with daily checks for leaks. However, flow spirometers generally require daily or twice-daily calibration checks. All spirometers must be recalibrated after cleaning or disinfection, or if an unusual or unexpected result indicates a problem.

Biological controls
In order to detect changes in overall spirometer performance, the ventilatory function of one or more subjects with stable respiratory function should be measured and recorded regularly as part of an ongoing quality control program. In the surgery, testing yourself (if you have stable function) on your spirometer every week is a practical way of monitoring

Table 3.1	Frequency of quality control (Miller et al. 2005b)
Test	**Frequency**
Volume	Daily
Leak	Daily
Volume linearity	Every 3 months
Flow linearity	Weekly
Time	Every 3 months

quality control. Generally, a variation of more than 5% in FEV_1 or FVC should alert you to a problem and the need to have your instrument properly checked and serviced. A practical approach is to measure the spirometry of the subject 10 times over a period of 2 to 3 weeks. From the results, calculate the mean and standard deviation for both FEV_1 and FVC. From these calculate the 95% confidence interval (mean ±1.96 × standard deviation). Any value for FEV_1 or FVC that subsequently falls outside these limits should alert you to the possibility that the spirometer has become inaccurate. The easiest way to handle serial data of this type is to plot it as a Levy–Jennings diagram as shown in Figure 3.3. Remember that testing a normal subject does not negate the need to calibrate (or to check the calibration of) the instrument regularly using a certified 3.00 litre syringe.

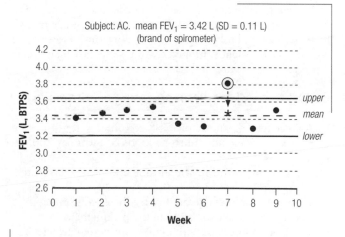

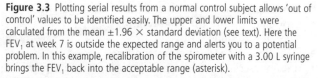

Figure 3.3 Plotting serial results from a normal control subject allows 'out of control' values to be identified easily. The upper and lower limits were calculated from the mean ±1.96 × standard deviation (see text). Here the FEV_1 at week 7 is outside the expected range and alerts you to a potential problem. In this example, recalibration of the spirometer with a 3.00 L syringe brings the FEV_1 back into the acceptable range (asterisk).

BTPS correction

It should be noted that if the accuracy of the spirometer is checked with a 3.00 litre syringe while the spirometer is in 'patient' rather than 'calibration' mode (if available), the volume recorded will usually be higher than the expected accuracy range of 2.895 to 3.105 litres. This is because in the patient-testing mode the spirometer will apply the BTPS correction factor (and possibly other factors, for example correction for gas viscosity). For a computerised volume-displacement spirometer, the recorded volume will be about 3.3 litres if the room temperature is 20°C.

When a volume-displacement spirometer is moved into a cooler or hotter environment, it is important to allow time for it to reach the new temperature and to measure it, otherwise the BTPS correction factor (see Appendix B) will be incorrect. Similarly, the calibration syringe needs to be at the same temperature as the spirometer and for this reason it is usually stored with the spirometer.

Mechanical peak flow meters can generally be expected to wear out after about 12 to 24 months of heavy use, although there is little published data to support this. However, a volume-displacement spirometer will usually last many years if properly maintained and serviced.

Factors to consider when choosing a spirometer

Factors governing the choice of spirometer for use in a doctor's surgery include (Burton, Johns & Swanney 2005):

- ease of use
- provision of easy to read real-time graphic display of the manoeuvre
- provision of immediate quality feedback concerning the acceptability of blows, including reproducibility
- provision to interface with clinical software packages
- provision of customisable final spirometry report
- provision to print the final report
- price and running costs
- reliability and ease of maintenance
- training, servicing and repair of the spirometer provided by the supplier

- ability to trial the spirometer in your setting before you purchase
- provision of a disposable sensor or a breathing circuit that can be easily cleaned and disinfected
- provision of appropriate normal reference values with lower limits of normal
- robustness
- provision of a comprehensive manual describing its operation, maintenance and calibration
- calibration requirements
- conforms to accepted spirometry performance standards (Appendix A)
- complies with electrical safety standards.

A summary of the specifications and features of spirometers on the market in Australia and New Zealand is provided in the *Spirometers Users' and Buyers' Guide* (Burton, Johns & Swanney 2005) posted at www.nationalasthma.org.au

Faced with the wide variety of spirometers available today, general practitioners have to choose an instrument suitable for use in their own surgery. If possible, trial the spirometer before buying to ensure it meets *your* specific needs.

Summary

All spirometers are regarded as diagnostic instruments and should meet or exceed relevant ERS/ATS (Miller et al. 2005b) equipment standards. Spirometers must be capable of being calibrated, or at least having their calibration checked, to ensure their ongoing accuracy. A 3.00 litre syringe is recommended for calibrating spirometers and this should be done regularly and the results recorded. To assess overall spirometer performance it is recommended that biological controls be included in the spirometer's quality assurance program with the results recorded in a table and Levy–Jennings plot. When purchasing a spirometer it is important that it meets or exceeds minimum performance criteria.

Chapter 4

How to do spirometry and the common problems

How to do spirometry

To ensure an acceptable result, the FVC manoeuvre must be performed with maximum effort immediately following a maximum inspiration; it should have a rapid start and the spirogram or flow-volume curve should be a smooth continuous curve throughout the manoeuvre. The test can be tiring for the elderly or breathless patient, so sufficient time for recovery should be allowed between repeat tests. It is important that the operator is properly trained before attempting to measure spirometry.

There are two breathing circuits commonly used when performing spirometry: closed- and open-circuit methods. The *open-circuit* method is used when the subject inspires fully before going onto the mouthpiece. The *closed-circuit* method requires the subject to first breathe tidally on the mouthpiece and then to inspire fully from the spirometer. The latter method has the advantage that the subject's inspired volume can be measured and is displayed, which can help to verify that the subject has inspired fully prior to performing the maximal manoeuvre of expiration-then-inspiration, and also has the advantage of being able to compare tidal with maximal breathing.

To achieve good results, carefully explain to the patient the procedure (be clear and precise) and what is being measured. Also ensure that he or she is sitting upright with feet firmly on the floor (the safest and most comfortable position; although standing and sitting give a similar result in adults, in children the vital capacity is usually greater in the standing position). Do not use a chair with wheels. Remember that verbal encouragement/coaching throughout the test is essential.

Open-circuit spirometry
Demonstrate the manoeuvre to the patient. Apply a nose-clip to the patient's nose (this is recommended, but not essential) and urge the patient to:
- breathe in fully (the subject should inspire rapidly until absolutely full)
- seal his or her lips around the mouthpiece and *immediately blast* the air out as fast and as far as possible until the lungs are *completely* empty (the patient should remain upright)
- breathe in again as forcibly and fully as possible (not all spirometers will measure inspiration).

Obtain at least three acceptable tests *then* apply the repeatability criteria (Table 4.1).

The measurement of IC using open-circuit spirometry involves switching the patient into this circuit at the end of quiet expiration (that is, FRC) and measuring the maximum volume that can be inspired (that is, to TLC).

Closed-circuit spirometry
Demonstrate the manoeuvre to the patient. Apply a nose-clip to the patient's nose (this is recommended, but not essential) and urge the patient to:
- seal his or her lips around the mouthpiece
- breath tidally for 2 to 4 breaths—usually until a stable FRC is recorded
- breathe in fully (the subject should inspire rapidly until absolutely full) and *immediately blast* the air out as fast and as far as possible until the lungs are *completely* empty (the patient should remain upright)
- breathe in again as forcibly and fully as possible (not all spirometers will measure inspiration).

Obtain at least three acceptable tests *then* apply the repeatability criteria (Table 4.1).

Closed-circuit spirometry facilitates the measurement of IC by affording the operator the capacity to scrutinise the stability of FRC during tidal breathing before asking the patient to inspire fully. Volume-displacement spirometers must contain a volume of air at the start of the manoeuvre that is greater than the patient's inspiratory capacity so that a full inspiratory breath can be measured.

Flow spirometers, provided they have the software to integrate inspiratory as well as expiratory flow, are usually more suitable as they do not require the patient to breathe in from an air reservoir.

Essentials of both open- and closed-circuit spirometry

For both methods, the *essentials* are: maximal inspiration; a good seal between the lips and mouthpiece; very vigorous effort right from the start of the manoeuvre, continuing until *absolutely* no more air can be exhaled; rapid start; the patient avoiding coughing, tongue occlusion, glottis closure, premature termination of the blow, etc. (see below); and the patient not leaning forward during the test. See also Table 4.1. The operator should be confident that the patient has followed the instructions. Note that failure to initially fill the lungs is a very common cause of poor quality spirometry.

Because the initial part of the expiration and all of the inspiration is effort-dependent, it is essential to achieve maximum patient effort in the performance of spirometry. Demonstrating to the patient the vigour and effort required is perhaps the best way to achieve this.

If only peak expiratory flow is being measured, the patient need only exhale for a couple of seconds.

Remember that, particularly in patients with airflow obstruction, it may take the patient many seconds to fully exhale. It is also important to recognise those patients whose efforts are submaximal. There is no substitute for careful explanation and demonstration—demonstrating the manoeuvre to the patient will overcome 90% of problems encountered and can be critical in achieving satisfactory results. Observation and encouragement of the patient's performance are also crucial. Be sure to examine the spirogram (or flow-volume curve) for acceptability and reproducibility and, if your spirometer doesn't do this for you, to correct the measurements to BTPS conditions (see Appendix B).

Measurements in young children

The measurement of spirometry in young children is a particular challenge and usually limited to those 5 years of age and older. It is important to present the child with a non-threatening environment, to minimise interruptions, to capture the child's imagination and to make spirometry fun. The instructions must be kept short and simple. Use body language and voice intonations to reinforce your instructions. Use very simple and understandable words and phrases such as 'blow like the big wolf' or 'blow the biggest mountain' and point to the flow-volume loop on the screen. Avoid words like 'inhale' and 'maximum' as a child may never have experienced these. As with adults, it usually helps to demonstrate the test. Children who are unable to perform satisfactory spirometry on their first visit often perform the test correctly at the next visit.

Acceptability criteria

At least three technically acceptable manoeuvres should be obtained which meet the ERS/ATS acceptability and repeatability criteria given in Table 4.1. It is important that the acceptability criteria be applied and unacceptable tests discarded before assessing repeatability, as the latter is used to determine whether additional tests from the three acceptable ones already obtained are required. These criteria (together with a properly maintained and calibrated spirometer) help to ensure the quality of your results which is essential when comparing results with predicted values and quantifying change over time. Tests which do not fully meet the acceptability criteria may still be clinically useful.

For example, FEV_1 may still be valid if cough or premature termination of the blow occurs after the first second. The report should state when the results are obtained from manoeuvres which do not meet acceptability and repeatability criteria.

Table 4.1	Acceptability criteria (Miller et al. 2005b)

Each individual test is acceptable if it meets the following criteria:

Start of test criteria (apply to each test)

- There was no evidence of hesitation
- The test was performed with a rapid start (that is, the extrapolated volume is less than 5% or 0.15 L, whichever is greater)
- The PEF has a sharp rise (flow-volume)

End of test criteria (apply to each test)

- Expiration continued until there was no change in volume (< 0.025 L) for ≥ 1 second, and the patient had blown for ≥ 3 seconds (children aged < 10 years) or for ≥ 6 seconds (subjects aged ≥ 10 years)
- (However, the patient or person conducting the test can terminate the blow if the patient cannot or should not continue)

Other criteria (apply to each test)

- The patient followed instructions
- A continuous maximal expiratory manoeuvre throughout the test (that is, no stops and starts) was achieved and was initiated from full inspiration
- There were no leaks
- No cough (note FEV_1 may be valid if cough occurs after the first second)
- No glottis closure (Valsalva)
- No obstruction of the mouthpiece (for example, by the tongue or teeth)
- No premature termination (note FEV_1 may be valid if this occurs after the first second)
- No evidence that the patient took an additional breath during the expiratory manoeuvre

Table 4.1 continued

Repeatability criteria

- Obtain three acceptable tests (that is, each test should meet the above acceptability criteria)
- The two largest values for FVC should agree to within 0.15 L
- The two largest values for FEV_1 should agree to within 0.15 L
- Repeat the test if these repeatability criteria are not met

Results to report

- FEV_1—report the largest value
- FVC—report the largest value
- PEF—report the largest value
- FEV_6—report the largest value
- FVC_6—report the largest value
- $FEF_{25-75\%}$—report the value obtained from the test with highest sum of FEV_1 + FVC

Back-extrapolation

Back-extrapolation is a procedure applied to the volume versus time curve to determine the appropriate time zero from which all timed volumes (for example, FEV_1) are calculated (Miller et al. 2005b). The derived time zero is the point on the time axis where exhalation would have started assuming 'instantaneous' flow acceleration (that is, the patient's maximal flow is projected back to the volume axis). The procedure minimises errors in the measurement of FEV_1 if the expiratory manoeuvre was not performed rapidly from the very start.

Back-extrapolation is quite simple. To calculate time zero, draw a line through the steepest portion of the volume-time curve and extend it back to the time axis. This point is taken as time zero (Figure 4.1). From this construction the 'extrapolated volume' can be calculated as shown in Figure 4.1. For an acceptably rapid start to the blow, the ERS/ATS requires that the extrapolated volume should be less than 5% FVC or 0.15 litres, whichever is greater. An extrapolated volume higher than this indicates that the blow was not initiated rapidly and should be repeated.

The back-extrapolation procedure is performed by hand with manual spirometers; however, in practice this is often only done when the spirogram shows an obvious slow start (that is, measurable extrapolated volume). Computerised spirometers that meet equipment standards (Miller et al. 2005b) will perform this procedure automatically, and many will provide immediate feedback if the extrapolated volume exceeds acceptable limits (that is, 5% FVC or 0.15 litres, whichever is greater).

Patient-related problems

It is useful to learn how to recognise inadequacies in the performance of spirometry and the recordings as these can greatly affect the accuracy, reproducibility and hence interpretation of the results. Figures 4.2 and 4.3 show some problematic examples compared with well-performed manoeuvres—illustrated for both the expiratory spirogram and the flow-volume loop.

As stated, optimum patient performance is crucial to obtaining valid spirometry. The patient must understand fully that the manoeuvre *must* be performed with maximal effort. If the test is performed correctly, the results from repeat blows will usually be reproducible (that is, FEV_1 and FVC to within 0.15 litres).

The most common patient-related problems when performing the FVC manoeuvre are:
- submaximal effort
- leaks between the lips and mouthpiece
- incomplete inspiration or expiration (prior to or during the forced manoeuvre)
- hesitation at the start of the expiration

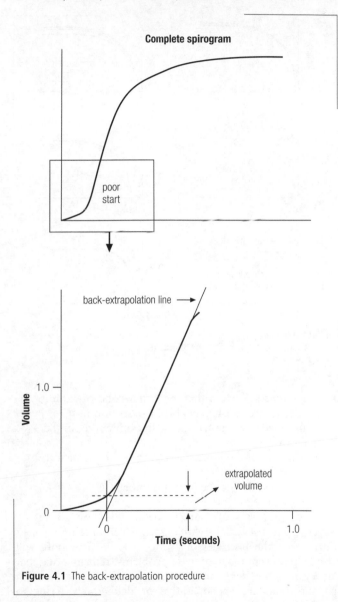

Figure 4.1 The back-extrapolation procedure

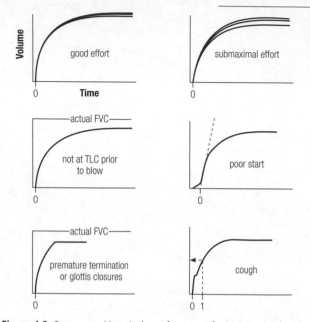

Figure 4.2 Common problems in the performance of spirometry are shown on these expiratory spirograms. The dotted line represents the acceptable maximal effort.

- cough (particularly within the first second of expiration)
- glottis closure causing an abrupt reduction in flow or straight sections (rather than a smooth curve) in the spirogram
- obstruction of the mouthpiece by the tongue or teeth (false or otherwise)
- vocalisation during the forced manoeuvre
- poor posture.

These problems can largely be avoided by giving the patient clear instructions with *vigorous* verbal reinforcement throughout the test. Demonstration of the procedure will also help prevent many of these problems, remembering that all effort-dependent measurements will be variable in patients who are uncooperative or deliberately trying to produce low values.

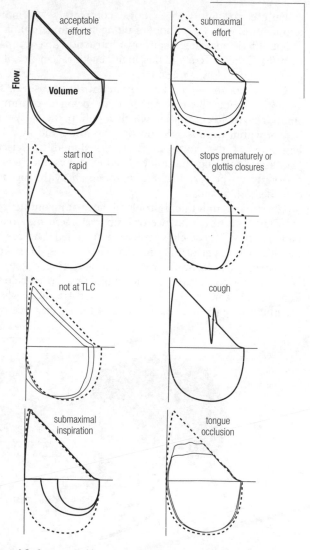

Figure 4.3 Common problems in the performance of spirometry are shown in these flow-volume loops. The dotted flow-volume loop represents the acceptable maximal effort.

Failure to empty the lungs completely (premature termination) is very common, resulting in an underestimation of both FVC and degree of airflow obstruction (overestimated FEV_1/FVC ratio). To avoid this, active encouragement right to the end of the blow is essential.

Glottis closure should be suspected if flow ceases or falls abruptly during the test rather than being a continuous smooth curve. Recordings in which cough, particularly if this occurs within the first second (it may affect the FEV_1), or hesitation at the start has occurred should be rejected. Vocalisation during the test will reduce flows and must be discouraged—performing the manoeuvre with the neck extended often helps.

Chest pain, abdominal problems, fear of incontinence or even just lack of confidence or embarrassment may reduce patient effort. Nose-clips are recommended but are not essential when performing forced manoeuvres. Discourage the patient from leaning forward during testing.

Modifying the cardboard mouthpiece as shown below in Figure 4.4 can generally prevent obstruction of the mouthpiece by the tongue. The end of the mouthpiece is cut

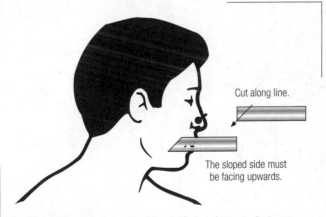

Cut along line.

The sloped side must be facing upwards.

Figure 4.4 Most mouthpieces can be modified as shown to eliminate occlusion of the mouthpiece by the tongue. Note that the sloped face of the mouthpiece *must* be positioned as shown.

or shaped at an angle of about 60° to its length and used with the *sloped side upward*, preventing obstruction by the tongue. Alternatively, the problem can be reduced significantly by instructing the subject to place the mouthpiece well into the mouth and to bite it lightly.

Instrument-related problems

These depend largely on the type of spirometer used but generally the most common problems are:
- leaks in the spirometer, breathing hose and hose connections (in volume-displacement spirometers)
- rips and tears in the flowhead connector tube (in flow spirometers)
- calibration, accuracy and linearity (in flow spirometers).

Standards recommend checking the calibration at least daily with a calibrated syringe; a simple self-test of the spirometer is an additional, useful daily check that the instrument is functioning correctly. Other faults may require repair by the manufacturer or distributor.

When using the volume-displacement spirometer that has a limited time axis (for example, the Vitalograph spirometer), it is very important to continue to record expired volume until the patient's lungs are empty and not to discontinue once the chart carrier stops moving, otherwise you will underestimate FVC and overestimate the FEV_1/FVC ratio. When using a volume-displacement spirometer that utilises a rotating drum (kymograph) to move the recording paper, it is important to allow the paper to reach the correct speed before the patient begins to blow. Therefore, switch on the kymograph a second or two before the patient blows.

Performing spirometry in the busy clinical practice

There is no doubt that spirometry is time-consuming, requiring about 20 minutes to perform, document and interpret pre- and post-bronchodilator measurements. This, together with the cost of purchasing and maintaining a spirometer, are arguments often put by general practitioners for not including spirometry as part of their general practice consultations. There are a number of ways to make testing more cost-effective (Fardy 2001):

- Perform pre-bronchodilator spirometry as soon as you have determined that your patient's problems may be related to asthma or COPD. Administer a bronchodilator and then complete the history-taking and clinical examination. By the time you have done this, sufficient time (10 minutes or more) will have passed for the post-bronchodilator blows to be done. With the results of spirometry now available, you will be better equipped to discuss the diagnosis, outlook and management plan with your patient. This strategy adds only about 10 minutes to your consultation but adds a lot of information that will be of immediate value and provide baseline measurements for future comparison (for example, effectiveness of treatment).
- Your practice nurse can measure the patient's spirometry for you, provided he or she has completed a comprehensive training course in spirometry.

Summary

Acceptable spirometry requires close cooperation between the patient and the operator in the performance of maximal breathing manoeuvres. Clear and concise instructions with constant encouragement from the operator are essential to obtain accurate and reproducible results. This is especially challenging in young children. At least three technically acceptable tests should be obtained and the FEV_1 and FVC in two of the three tests should vary by less than 0.15 litres. The highest FEV_1 and FVC (even if from separate blows) are reported. The quoted $FEF_{25-75\%}$ should be calculated from the single blow with the highest sum of FEV_1 plus FVC. A range of patient- and instrument-related problems can affect the results but most of these can be easily identified and avoided.

PART 2

Chapter 5

Infection control

Cross-infection and lung function testing

Although there is little evidence of direct transmission of disease via lung function equipment, there is evidence that pathogenic organisms can contaminate lung function equipment thus posing a risk of cross-infection between patients (Unstead et al. 2006; Miller et al. 2005a). During spirometry patients can generate flows up to 14 L/s (840 L/min) which can easily mobilise saliva and create dense macro- and micro-aerosols by entrainment of the fluid lining the mucous membranes. These can then be deposited in the equipment. Unless such deposition is prevented or the equipment is rigorously cleaned and decontaminated between patients, the chance of cross-infection exists. This is particularly important today where our patients range from healthy to the more immunosuppressed (due to illness or treatment) where the likelihood of cross-infection may be increased.

Although the transmission of respiratory pathogens (for example *Mycobacterium avium*, *M. tuberculosis* and *Aspergillus* species) via spirometers has not been fully established, the potential risks are difficult to disprove. However, it has been established that organisms such as *Pseudomonas*, *Burkholderia cepacia*, *Haemophilus influenzae* and acid-fast bacillae can be recovered from spirometers.

A comprehensive review of the potential sources and risks of cross-infection during lung function testing and the methods available for disinfection and sterilisation and practical recommendations has been published (Kendrick, Johns & Leeming 2003).

Reducing the risk of cross-infection

In patients with a known infectious disease, many laboratories prefer to measure ventilatory function using a pneumotachograph or other electronic sensor, as these can be more easily and effectively cleaned and sterilised than conventional bellows or water-sealed spirometers which have nooks and crannies in which organisms may flourish. Since it is usually impractical to decontaminate the interior surfaces of a spirometer between patients effectively, most lung function laboratories clean and disinfect their equipment periodically (weekly or monthly). The efficacy of decontamination protocols at reducing the risk of cross-infection has not been documented and the risk certainly remains if decontamination of the equipment is not carried out after each patient. Spirometers will usually require recalibration (or that the calibration be checked) after cleaning and decontamination.

If you are disassembling the spirometer for cleaning, it is essential to:
• thoroughly clean and decontaminate the components
• thoroughly dry the components before reassembling
• check the spirometer for correct operation
• check and, if necessary, adjust the calibration.

Mouthpieces must be disposed of or cleaned and disinfected between patients because the greatest danger of cross-infection is via direct contact with bodily fluids.

An alternative approach which is now widespread is the use of a disposable (single patient use) barrier filter. This is attached to the mouthpiece of the spirometer and the patient performs the breathing manoeuvre through it to minimise the risk of equipment contamination. These filters have a low resistance to flow and do not significantly affect the clinical measurements of ventilatory function, except perhaps PEF (Johns et al. 1995). The effectiveness of some of these filters at removing bacteria and viruses has been questioned, particularly when used with patients who can generate high flows (more than 700 L/min). The best filter medium available has been shown to offer a 99.7% filtration efficiency, which implies more than 99.99% cross-contamination reduction efficiency. This is probably a similar degree of protection to that offered by wet cleaning and decontaminating equipment between patients. A recent study has shown that barrier filters are effective at preventing the contamination and hence reducing the risk of cross-infection during lung function testing (Unstead et al. 2006). Filters also have the advantage of protecting delicate sensors and the internal surfaces of the spirometer from damage, and reduce the corroding effects of cleaning agents and disinfectants. The extent to which the use of filters can effectively obviate the need for cleaning and disinfection is unclear. The cost of filters may be less than the cleaning and disinfection costs (Side et al. 1999), particularly in the setting of a lung function laboratory.

Other laboratories use disposable mouthpieces containing a one-way valve to prevent inspiration from equipment. Disposable mouthpieces cannot be used with spirometers requiring an initial period of tidal breathing. However, they can be used only when performing solely expiratory spirometry and it is doubtful that they would be effective at reducing the risk of cross-infection. When using one-way mouthpieces, it is important to ensure that the patient has *fully* inspired *before* placing the mouthpiece in the mouth, as further inspiration will be prevented.

Studies documenting the risk of developing clinically relevant infection from spirometry equipment and the extent to which cleaning, disinfection or the use of filters are protective are urgently needed to provide an evidence base for clinical practice.

Summary

Although there is little direct evidence of disease transmission via lung function equipment, precautions should be taken to minimise any risk. Mouthpieces must either be cleaned and disinfected between patients, or discarded. The interior and exterior surfaces of the spirometer should be decontaminated regularly. An alternative approach, which is becoming common practice in some countries, is the use of disposable, low-resistance barrier filters which have the additional function of protecting the equipment. Also, disposable mouthpieces incorporating a one-way valve are used when only expiratory manoeuvres are performed to prevent the patient inspiring from the spirometer.

Chapter 6

Predicted normal values

Normal values

To interpret ventilatory function tests in any individual, their results need to be compared with reference values obtained from a well-defined population of normal subjects matched for gender, age, height and ethnic origin and using:
- similar test protocols, and
- carefully calibrated and validated instruments.

Normal predicted values for ventilatory function generally vary as follows:

Gender: For a given height and age, males have a larger FEV_1, FVC, $FEF_{25-75\%}$ and PEF but a slightly lower FEV_1/FVC ratio.

Age: FEV_1, FVC, $FEF_{25-75\%}$ and PEF increase with age until about 18 years in females and 20 years in males. After this, all indices gradually fall, although the precise rate of decline is probably masked due to the complex interrelationship between age and height. The fall in the FEV_1/FVC ratio with age in adults is due to the greater decline in FEV_1 than in FVC. A large change in predicted values can occur from the transition from adolescent to adult when predicted data is obtained from separate studies.

Height: All indices other than the FEV_1/FVC ratio
               increase with standing height. Arm span
               (fingertip to fingertip) may be used if the
               subject is unable to stand or has spinal
               deformity.

Ethnic origin: Caucasians have the largest FEV_1 and FVC
               and, of the various ethnic groups, Polynesians
               are among the lowest. The values for black
               Africans are 10–15% lower than for
               Caucasians of similar age, sex and height
               because, for a given standing height, their
               thorax is shorter. Chinese have been found to
               have an FVC about 20% lower and Indians
               about 10% lower than matched Caucasians.
               There is little difference in PEF between ethnic
               groups. The FEV_1/FVC ratio is similar
               between ethnic groups. Many lung function
               laboratories use Caucasian predicted values
               and apply a factor (for example × 0.88) to
               correct for ethnic differences.

Body weight is not a strong predictor of lung size except
in subjects who are significantly under- or overweight, in
which case it is usually low.

There is a vast literature of normal population studies,
many of which have deficiencies in sample size, ethnicity,
definition of normality, inclusion of smokers and choice of
equipment. The most appropriate predicted values will be
influenced by the community in which you are working. In
the absence of population-specific reference values,
Mediterranean values are better predicted by European ones
and Australian values are better predicted by American ones.

Appendix C provides tables of mean predicted values and
lower limits of normal (LLN) for Caucasians of both genders
for FEV_1, FVC, FEV_1/FVC, $FEF_{25-75\%}$, PEF, FVC_6,
FEV_1/FVC_6 and $FEF_{25-75\%6}$. The tables are based on a large
and well-conducted study of asymptomatic, lifelong non-
smokers (aged 8 to 80 years) who participated in the
National Health and Nutrition Examination Survey
(NHANES III) (Hankinson, Odencrantz & Fedan 1999;
Hankinson, Crapo & Jensen 2003). Normal values for IC

can be obtained by subtracting predicted FRC from predicted TLC. Suitable reference equations for predicting FRC and TLC are available from Quanjer et al. (1993). It is not recommended to extrapolate beyond the age and height range of the population used to obtain the reference equations used.

Ventilatory abnormalities can be inferred if any of FEV_1, FVC, PEF and the FEV_1/FVC ratio are below the lower limit of normal. The *lower* limit of normal can be defined by the 95% confidence interval, which for normally distributed data is 1.64 standard errors below the mean predicted value for these indices (that is, 5% of the healthy population will be classified as abnormal). An *upper* limit of normal is not usually used because *disease usually only decreases* their value. For the FEV_1/FVC ratio, disease can both increase and decrease it, so the normal *range* is sometimes used as mean ±1.96 standard deviations. The use of a fixed value for the lower limit (for example 80% of the mean predicted for FEV_1 and FVC, and 70% for the FEV_1/FVC ratio) is *not recommended* as this can result in false positives in older people and false negatives in young adults. This is illustrated in Figures 6.1 and 6.2 for FEV_1 and the FEV_1/FVC ratio where the use of a fixed lower limit value (dotted line in these figures) is clearly inappropriate.

Selecting the most appropriate normal values

The best advice is to seek guidance from your local hospital-based lung function laboratory. We believe that the predicted values published by Hankinson, Odencrantz and Fedan (1999) and Hankinson, Crapo and Jensen (2003) are the most appropriate for general use in Australia and New Zealand (see Appendix C).

If you want to select your own normal value set, then one approach involves reviewing the available literature against a checklist of specific acceptability criteria. Acceptability criteria may include:

• Were the subjects randomly selected from the general population (no bias) and of the required ethnic group?

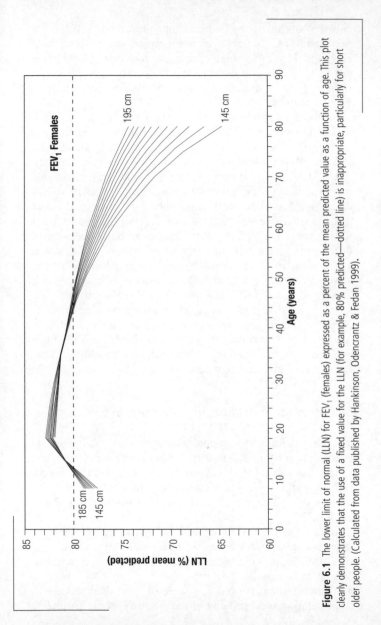

Figure 6.1 The lower limit of normal (LLN) for FEV$_1$ (females) expressed as a percent of the mean predicted value as a function of age. This plot clearly demonstrates that the use of a fixed value for the LLN (for example, 80% predicted—dotted line) is inappropriate, particularly for short older people. (Calculated from data published by Hankinson, Odencrantz & Fedan 1999).

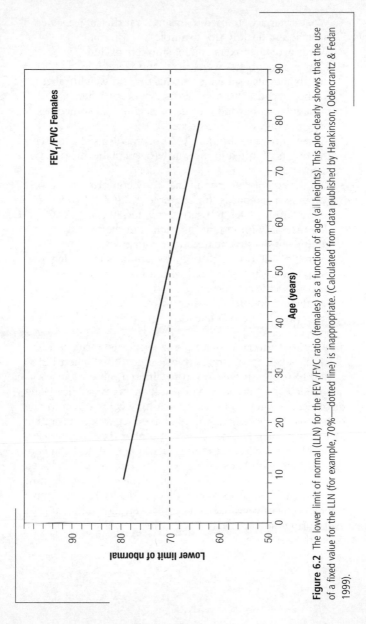

Figure 6.2 The lower limit of normal (LLN) for the FEV_1/FVC ratio (females) as a function of age (all heights). This plot clearly shows that the use of a fixed value for the LLN (for example, 70%—dotted line) is inappropriate. (Calculated from data published by Hankinson, Odencrantz & Fedan 1999).

- What criteria were used to ensure that the subjects were normal and healthy (for example, no asthma)?
- Were current smokers and ex-smokers excluded?
- How many subjects were there, and were they distributed across a wide age, height and weight range for both genders? (Large errors can occur when extrapolating beyond the age or height, and sometimes weight, range of subjects tested.)
- Were rigorous calibration (QA) protocols used and were the results reported in the study (or available on request)?
- Did the equipment used in the study conform to recognised standards (for example, ERS/ATS [Miller et al. 2005b] for back pressure, accuracy, linear range)?
- Are there any important differences in the type(s) of equipment used compared with your own? (For example, PEF can be different when measured using a peak flow meter compared with a flow or volume-displacement spirometer.)
- Do the methodologies match those used in your laboratory? (For example, do they apply the ATS and ERS guidelines?)
- Were the criteria for selecting the reported results the same as your own (for example, report the highest FEV_1 and FVC even if they are from different blows)?

In our experience this will result in many studies being discarded, leaving a shortlist which may come down to one or two papers, particularly if you have used a rigorous rating system. It is then helpful to test a number (for example, 20) of healthy subjects of various ages and heights and compare their results with those given on the remaining published studies. It is then reasonable to select the study which most closely matches (for example, FEV_1 and FVC) your sample population. However, it has recently been shown that at least 100 normal subjects may need to be tested to confidently make this selection.

Summary

The results of spirometry (for example FEV_1, FVC) are usually compared with predicted values based on the patient's age, height, gender and ethnic origin. Most computerised diagnostic spirometers allow the operator to select from a number of normal value studies and some allow custom equations to be entered. The choice of the most appropriate equations to use can be difficult and a rationale to help in the selection is given. A commonly used set of predicted lung function values is given in Appendix C.

PART 3

Chapter 7

Interpretation of ventilatory function tests

Measurements of ventilatory function may be very useful in a diagnostic sense but they are also useful in following the natural history of disease over a period of time, assessing preoperative risk and quantifying the effects of treatment. The presence of ventilatory abnormality can be inferred if one or more of FEV_1, VC, $FEF_{25-75\%}$, PEF or the FEV_1/FVC ratio is below the normal range or in the presence of an abnormal shape of the flow-volume loop.

Significant change in spirometry with time

Serial measurements of ventilatory function can provide important information about disease progression and response to therapy. However, it is often difficult to decide what constitutes a significant change as this varies depending on the index (FEV_1, FVC, etc.) and the time interval between repeat measurements, and may differ in disease and healthy subjects. Table 7.1 provides recommended guidelines as to what constitutes a significant change over several time periods (Pellegrino et al. 2005).

Thus, changes greater than those given in Table 7.1 would need to occur to have confidence that the change was real. The ERS/ATS suggest that for FEV_1 short-term changes of > 12% and > 0.2 L may be clinically important (Pellegrino et al. 2005). This would be particularly true if on each occasion

Table 7.1	Percentage changes required to be significant (Pellegrino et al. 2005)		
	FVC	FEV_1	$FEF_{25-75\%}$
Day to day			
Normal subjects	≥5	≥5	≥13
COPD	≥11	≥13	≥23
Week to week			
Normal subjects	≥11	≥12	≥21
COPD	≥20	≥20	≥30
Year to year	≥15	≥15	

the FEV_1 was repeatable. This illustrates the importance of obtaining measurements of high quality.

The rate of fall of FEV_1 over time is an important indicator of disease progression in people with COPD. In healthy, non-smoking adults the decrease is about 30 mL/year with an upper limit of about 50 mL/year (Ferguson et al. 2000). A decrease greater than this suggests an abnormally rapid rate of deterioration, presumably due to the progression of the disease. However, determining the rate of decline in a patient is not easy because it requires monitoring over years and can be greatly affected by changes in equipment performance and the quality of spirometry.

Classifying abnormal ventilatory function

There are three classifications for abnormal ventilatory function (see Table 7.2 and Figure 7.1):
1. **Obstructive ventilatory defect:** characterised by airflow limitation, for example reduced FEV_1, FEV_1/FVC ratio or PEF. An FEV_1/FVC ratio below the lower limit of normal is often used to *detect* obstruction and the FEV_1 expressed as a percent of the mean predicted value to *grade* its severity. (The term 'obstructive' is often used in this book as it is in common use. 'Airflow limitation' is a more accurate term as it recognises that reduced expiratory

Table 7.2		Classification of ventilatory abnormalities by spirometry	
	Obstructive	Apparent restrictive	Mixed
FEV$_1$	↓	↓ or N	↓
FVC	↓ or N	↓	↓
FEV$_1$/FVC	↓	↑ or N	↓

flows may be a consequence not only of airway narrowing (due to airway wall inflammation, mucus and so on) but also of dynamic airway collapse due to loss of radial traction to the airway wall as a consequence of parenchymal destruction.)

2. **Restrictive ventilatory defect**: characterised by loss of lung volume in the absence of airflow limitation, as suggested by a low VC or FVC but normal or high FEV$_1$/FVC ratio.

3. **Mixed obstructive and restrictive ventilatory defect**: characterised by both airflow limitation *and* loss of lung volume; that is, a low FEV$_1$/FVC ratio and low VC. Total lung capacity needs to be measured to confirm the restrictive component because loss of FVC and VC can occur in the presence of hyperinflation in diseases causing airflow limitation.

The interrelationships between the various measurements are important diagnostically (see Table 7.2 and Figures 7.1 and 7.2). For example:

- A reduction of FEV$_1$ in relation to the forced vital capacity will result in a low FEV$_1$/FVC ratio and is typical of *obstructive ventilatory defects* (for example asthma, chronic airways disease and emphysema). The lower limit of normal for the FEV$_1$/FVC ratio is around 70% but the exact lower limit is dependent on age as shown in Figure 6.2 for females. The predicted normal values by age, sex and height are given in the tables in Appendix C. In obstructive lung disease the FVC may be less than the slow VC because of airway closure occurring earlier during the forced manoeuvre. This may lead to an overestimation of the FEV$_1$/FVC

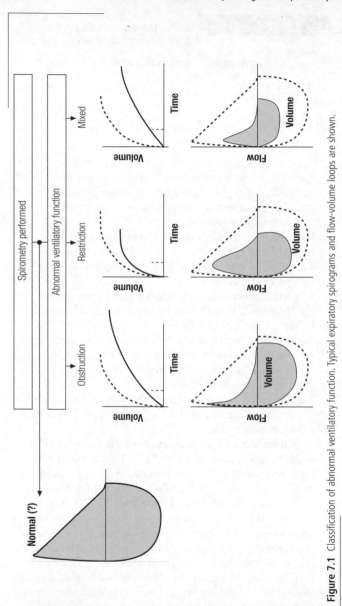

Figure 7.1 Classification of abnormal ventilatory function. Typical expiratory spirograms and flow-volume loops are shown.

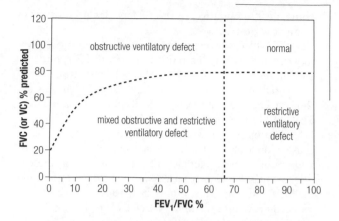

Figure 7.2 Plot of FVC or VC (spirometric index of lung 'size'), expressed as percentage predicted, and the FEV$_1$/FVC ratio (index of obstruction) to illustrate the interpretation of spirometry. The vertical dotted line represents the patient's (male, aged 60 years, height 170 cm) lower limit of normal for FEV$_1$/FVC ratio (varies with age and gender) and the horizontal dotted line is the lower limit of normal for FVC or VC (varies with age, gender and height). The position of the curved dotted line can vary but illustrates that with increasing airflow obstruction the FVC (or VC) is often reduced due to excessive airway narrowing and closure during the forced expiration and not due to 'small' lungs.

ratio. Thus, the FEV$_1$/VC ratio may be a more sensitive index for identifying airflow obstruction. It has been shown that in patients with known lung disease a reduced FEV$_1$/VC ratio predicts morbidity and mortality even when the FEV$_1$ is normal. However, in healthy people the meaning of a low ratio in the presence of a normal FEV$_1$ is uncertain (Pellegrino et al. 2005).

An *obstructive ventilatory defect* may also be inferred if the FEF$_{25-75\%}$ is less than the lower limit of normal, even if the FEV$_1$ is normal. This result suggests that the site of obstruction is the peripheral or small airways. It should be noted that the FEF$_{25-75\%}$ can be confidently compared with predicted normal values only if the FVC is normal. Similarly, serial measurements of FEF$_{25-75\%}$ are meaningful only if the FVC remains constant. Prolongation of the FET is also an indication of airflow obstruction.

- The FEV_1/FVC ratio remains normal or high (typically, more than 80%) with a reduction in both FEV_1 and FVC in *restrictive ventilatory defects* (for example interstitial lung disease, respiratory muscle weakness and thoracic cage deformities such as kyphoscoliosis). The FEV_1/FVC ratio may also be slightly low in tall, lean, healthy subjects whose chest is long and narrow. The cause is unclear, but it may be because airway calibre is a function of chest diameter; thus the airways in these subjects may be slightly narrower than normal and limit the FEV_1. Alternatively, it may be a consequence of reduced growth of the airways relative to the lung parenchyma or alveolar tissue.

- A reduced FVC together with a low FEV_1/FVC ratio is a feature of a *mixed ventilatory defect* in which a combination of both obstruction and restriction appears to be present. Alternatively, this may occur in airflow obstruction as a consequence of airway closure resulting in gas trapping, rather than as a result of small lungs. It is necessary to measure the patient's total lung capacity to distinguish between these two possibilities and to quantify the restrictive component.

The shape of the expiratory flow-volume curve varies between *obstructive ventilatory defects* where maximal flow rates are diminished and the expiratory curve is scooped out or convex towards the flow and volume axes, and *restrictive diseases* where expiratory flows may be increased in relation to lung volume and the shape often convex away from the axes. Diminished flows on the expiratory curve as residual volume is approached are suggestive of obstruction in the small peripheral airways. Examination of the shape of the flow-volume loop can help to distinguish different disease states (Figure 7.3).

However, note that the inspiratory curve is effort-dependent and thus very sensitive to submaximal effort, whereas the expiratory curve is largely independent of effort. Severe emphysema often causes a very rapid decrease in expiratory flow which is dependent on

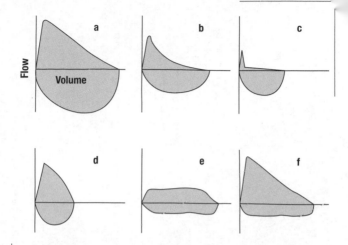

Figure 7.3 The normal flow-volume loop is shown together with examples of how respiratory disease can alter its shape. (a) Normal subject (b) Obstructive airway disease (for example, asthma) (c) Severe obstructive disease (for example, emphysema) (d) Restrictive lung disease (for example, pulmonary fibrosis) (e) Fixed major airway obstruction (for example, carcinoma of the trachea) (f) Floppy extra-thoracic airway obstruction (for example, tracheomalacia)

expiratory effort whereas inspiratory flow is well preserved (Figure 7.3(c)). In emphysema, the airways are prone to rapid collapse and/or narrowing during forced expiration (pressure-dependent) due to loss of elastic tissue airway support with the obliteration of the alveolar walls. During inspiration, the airways are easily dilated, preserving inspiratory flows. If the airflow limitation is due to airways disease (for example, asthma), the scalloping of the expiratory curve is more gradual and less effort-dependent (volume-dependent collapse). The inspiratory flows are also reduced, suggesting that the cause of the airflow limitation is relatively 'fixed'.

Truncation of inspiratory flow may result from a floppy extra-thoracic airway (for example, tracheomalacia of the larynx, fractured larynx), whereas both inspiratory and expiratory flows are truncated for fixed lesions (for example, carcinoma of the trachea). Expiratory flows alone may be

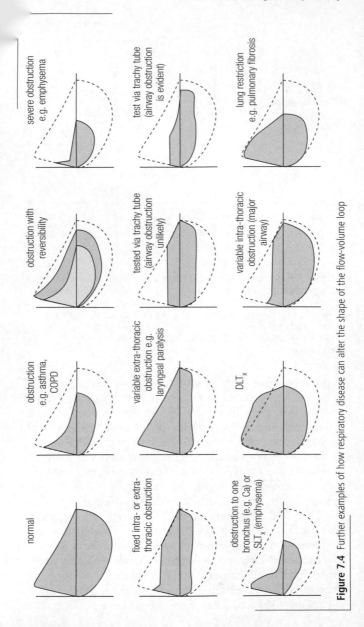

Figure 7.4 Further examples of how respiratory disease can alter the shape of the flow-volume loop

reduced for intra-thoracic lesions of the large airways (for example, tracheomalacia of the lower trachea and main bronchi). Further examples of the different flow-volume loop shapes are given in Figure 7.4.

The flow-volume loop is also useful for assessing ventilatory impairment during exercise. The tidal volume and inspiratory and expiratory flows increase with exercise but *are constrained within the boundary of the maximum flow-volume loop*. In the presence of airflow limitation, the patient's capacity to increase ventilation to meet the body's increased metabolic demands during exercise is limited. This is illustrated in Figure 7.5 where the capacity to exercise will be clearly impaired due to reduced capacity to ventilate—a consequence of the curvilinearity in the maximal expiratory flow-volume curve. Once tidal breathing hits the boundary of the flow-volume curve, the only way to further increase ventilation is for the patient to breathe at a higher lung volume where there is more 'room' to ventilate. In exercise, expiratory time becomes reduced and this tends to increase functional residual capacity, yet tidal volume is increased so that end-expiratory volume is even further increased compared with its resting or quiet breathing level. The increase in end-expiratory volume (FRC) can be measured as a decrease in inspiratory capacity. Patients with severe airflow obstruction thus

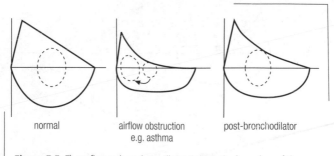

| normal | airflow obstruction e.g. asthma | post-bronchodilator |

Figure 7.5 These flow-volume loops illustrate how the boundary of the maximum loop can limit minute ventilation and thereby impede exercise tolerance (see text). The dotted loops represent tidal breathing at rest and during exercise.

develop dynamic hyperinflation during exercise and this expands the envelope of flow rates achievable within the tidal breathing range.

Inspiratory capacity (IC) is a measure of the maximum volume which can be inspired from FRC to TLC. The IC is reduced both in obstructive diseases when hyperinflation is present (Figure 7.6) and in restrictive disease when total lung capacity is reduced. When airflow obstruction has been identified by reductions in FEV_1, FVC and FEV_1/FVC, the IC affords a good measure of hyperinflation and is reduced in airways disease because FRC is increased. Hyperinflation may be chronic and stable as in emphysema but may increase with exercise or acute worsening of airflow obstruction. It may improve with bronchodilation or with oxygen therapy, which reduces ventilatory equivalents and permits slower breathing with more time for expirations so that a lower end-expiratory lung volume is achieved.

There is currently much interest in the measurement of IC, both during quiet breathing and developing dynamically during exercise, as a sensitive marker of change and

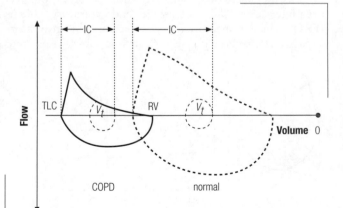

Figure 7.6 Flow-volume curve from a patient with COPD (predicted curve is dotted), showing displacement to the left (hyperinflation), limited tidal flows and reduced inspiratory capacity

treatment response in COPD because changes in dynamic hyperinflation may occur without much change in maximal expired volumes, for example FEV_1 and FVC.

Although the measurement of IC in clinical practice requires further evaluation, it may well prove of clinical utility in assessing progress and treatment response in the individual with COPD. Recent research has shown that IC correlates better than FEV_1, FVC, etc. with improvement in dyspnoea, exercise tolerance and quality of life measures in the disease.

Grading severity of a ventilatory defect

There are currently no universally accepted criteria for rating the severity of ventilatory defects. However, FEV_1 expressed as a percentage of the mean predicted value is usually used to grade the severity of obstructive defects and VC (or FVC) in the absence of obstruction (i.e. when FEV_1/FVC is normal) for estimating the severity of lung restriction. Table 7.3 has suggested a grading system based on clinical experience. Note that in patients with upper airway obstruction (for example, tracheal stenosis) the use of FEV_1 % predicted to grade the severity of an obstructive defect may result in underestimation of severity and is not recommended (Pellegrino et al. 2005). The use of the FEV_1/FVC ratio to grade obstruction is not generally recommended because obstructive lung disease can reduce both FEV_1 and FVC and also the ratio does not provide any information about the absolute values which determine the capacity to ventilate and degree of respiratory impairment. A reduced $FEF_{25-75\%}$ in the presence of a normal FEV_1, FVC and FEV_1/FVC is usually regarded as an indication of a mild obstructive defect.

Measuring reversibility of airflow obstruction

To measure the degree of reversibility (typically increased in asthma) of airflow obstruction, perform spirometry before and 10 to 15 minutes after administering a bronchodilator

Table 7.3

1. Grading the severity of an obstructive ventilatory defect

FEV$_1$ % predicted	Severity grading
> 70	Mild obstructive defect
60–69	Moderate obstructive defect
50–59	Moderately severe obstructive defect
35–49	Severe obstructive defect
< 35	Very severe obstructive defect

2. Grading the severity of an apparent restrictive ventilatory defect

VC (or FVC) % predicted	FEV$_1$/FVC ratio	Severity grading*
> 80	Normal	Probably normal
70–80	Normal	Mild restrictive defect
60–70	Normal	Moderate restrictive defect
< 60	Normal	Severe restrictive defect

* Need to confirm restriction by measuring lung volumes

by metered dose inhaler or jet nebuliser. Short-acting β-agonists (for example albutamol/salbutamol or terbutaline) are generally considered the benchmark bronchodilators for reversibility testing. If slower-acting agents (such as ipratropium bromide) are used, the post-bronchodilator test should be conducted at least 30 minutes after its administration.

The FEV$_1$ is the most common index used to quantify the degree of improvement. To determine the degree of improvement, calculate the following:
- the *absolute change* in FEV$_1$ (post-bronchodilator FEV$_1$ minus baseline FEV$_1$), and
- the *percentage increase* from the baseline FEV$_1$:

$$\% \text{ improvement} = 100 \times \frac{\text{FEV}_1 \text{ (post-bronchodilator)} - \text{FEV}_1 \text{ (baseline)}}{\text{FEV}_1 \text{ (baseline)}}$$

There is presently no universal agreement on the definition of significant bronchodilator reversibility. According to the ERS/ATS, the criteria for a positive response in adults are (Pellegrino et al. 2005):

Increase in FEV_1 (and/or FVC) from baseline $\geq 12\%$ and ≥ 0.2 L

If possible the patient should not use their short-acting bronchodilator (for example albutamol/salbutamol, ipratropium bromide) within four hours of testing. Long-acting inhaled bronchodilators (for example salmeterol) should be withheld for 12 hours prior to reversibility testing.

The most common method for administering the inhaled bronchodilator for reversibility testing is via a valved spacer. When albutamol/salbutamol is used it is common to administer 4 separate doses of 100 µg (total 400 µg), allowing a 30 second interval between each dose.

Normal subjects generally exhibit a smaller degree of reversibility (up to 8% in most studies). The absence of reversibility does not exclude asthma because an asthmatic's response can vary from time to time and at times airway calibre in asthmatic subjects is clearly normal and incapable of dramatic improvement. Also, the post-bronchodilator spirometry may not have been done at the optimum time when peak response occurs and in some patients the forced expiratory manoeuvre may cause compression of airways which may mask underlying improvement.

Bronchodilator response based on an improvement in $FEF_{25-75\%}$ can be difficult to interpret as it varies with FVC which is often larger post-bronchodilator. Thus, it is not recommended that $FEF_{25-75\%}$ be used to assess reversibility. Assessment of improvement in IC post-bronchodilator (often paralleling improvement in symptoms), indicating a decreased degree of hyperinflation, may be an important indicator of significant response even when FEV_1 is unchanged in patients with COPD. This illustrates the complexity of assessing bronchodilator response and that reliance on the change in FEV_1 (or FVC) alone can be inadequate and should not necessarily preclude prescribing a bronchodilator on a trial basis. This measurement of IC is not commonly made in general practice at present but may be of clinical value and may become more utilised in the future.

Accurate and reproducible measurements can be influenced by the amount of bronchodilator delivered to the airways. Studies have demonstrated that a reduced amount of bronchodilator to the airways can result in less than maximal bronchodilator improvement. As a result, patients tested would not demonstrate the optimal result that the bronchodilator could deliver.

If a metered dose inhaler is to be used, carefully check the subject's inhaler technique. About 30% of adults and 50% of children do not use their metered dose inhalers correctly. If this is so, the use of a valved spacer device or jet nebuliser to improve aerosol delivery would be appropriate.

It should be noted that on rare occasions a paradoxical response to a bronchodilator might occur in which the drug causes airway narrowing.

Airway provocation testing

The measurement of airway hyperresponsiveness is not commonly performed in a doctor's surgery and will not be discussed in detail.

The airway provocation test is used to detect and quantify airway hyperreactivity, an important feature of clinical asthma and, quantitatively, airway hyperresponsiveness is thought to reflect asthma severity. However, some asthmatics may have a negative challenge, particularly if treated with corticosteroids, and normal subjects with no history of asthma or variability in spirometry may return positive challenge results, particularly following recent upper respiratory tract infection.

In this test the patient is exposed to a stimulus that may induce bronchospasm, such as:

- exercise
- isocapnic hyperventilation
- hypertonic saline aerosol

- allergens and occupational inhalants
- methacholine aerosol
- histamine aerosol
- mannitol aerosol.

The test involves measuring spirometry at baseline and then at intervals following the stimuli. Unlike measuring bronchodilator response, here the effect of the stimulus is to decrease ventilatory function. The most common bronchial provocation agent is methacholine, which is delivered to the airway as an aerosol and stimulates cholinergic receptors in airway smooth muscle. Progressively increasing doses of methacholine are administered with measurements of FEV_1 between each dose. The test is positive and terminated when the FEV_1 falls by 20% from the baseline value (called the provoking dose, $PD_{20\%}$—see Figure 7.7). A positive response indicates heightened airway reactivity (airway narrowing in response to the stimulus). This is characteristic of bronchial asthma but also occurs to a lesser extent in chronic obstructive pulmonary disease and following respiratory infection in otherwise normal individuals. Treatment with

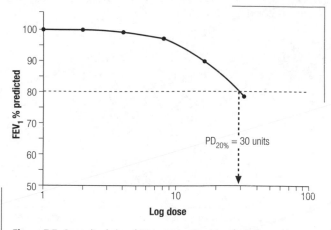

Figure 7.7 Generalised plot of FEV_1 versus provoking dose. The test is terminated when the FEV_1 falls by 20% from the baseline value; the concentration or dose of agent causing this degree of fall is reported as the $PD_{20\%}$.

anti-inflammatory agents may suppress bronchial reactivity in patients with asthma, resulting in a shift of the provocation curve to the right or an increase in the dose of provoking agent necessary to produce a given level of bronchoconstriction.

Peak flow monitoring

The availability of inexpensive peak flow meters has allowed the physician to directly involve patients in the management of their disease by self-monitoring of airway function. This is particularly so in asthma where regular peak flow monitoring is commonly part of a written management plan negotiated between the patient and his or her doctor. It is also particularly useful for the assessment of occupational asthma, where PEF readings performed at work are compared with baseline readings recorded during periods off work and may reveal a clear relationship between work exposure and bronchoconstriction, with recovery on weekends, holidays and so on, or with treatment. A typical record is given in Figure 7.8.

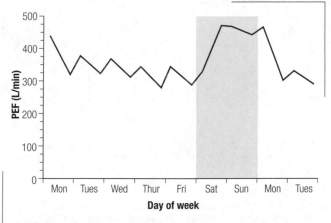

Figure 7.8 Self-monitoring of PEF during 7 days in a worker who attends work Monday to Friday with weekends off. Note that the PEF increases at the weekends when the worker is not at work.

Measurement of peak expiratory flow is simpler than spirometry. Its limitations are that it is effort-dependent, insensitive to obstructions of small and peripheral airways and that the inter- and intra-subject variability is about twice that of FEV_1. This is particularly true in children where PEF can be unreliable as they are often unable to perform the test with consistent maximal efforts. Also, diurnal variation, even in healthy children, can be as high as 30% (National Asthma Council Australia, 2006). The physician should provide the patient with clear, written instructions about how to perform and record his or her PEF. It is essential to stress the importance of accurate recordings of PEF and to motivate the patient.

When peak expiratory flow is measured repeatedly over a period and plotted against time (for example, by asthmatic patients), the pattern of the graph can be very important in identifying particular aspects of the patient's disease. Typical patterns are:

- the fall in PEF during the week with improvement on weekends and holidays which occurs in occupational asthma (Figure 7.8), and
- the 'morning dipper' pattern of some asthmatic patients caused by a fall in PEF in the early morning hours (Figure 7.9). Isolated falls in PEF in relation to specific allergens or trigger factors can help to identify and quantify these for the doctor and patient. A downward trend in PEF and an increase in its variability can identify worsening asthma and can be used to guide therapy, a strategy recommended by the National Asthma Council of Australia (2006). PEF monitoring is particularly useful in the substantial number of asthmatic people with poor perception of their own airway calibre. Response to asthma treatment is usually accompanied by an increase in PEF and a decrease in its variability.

Remember that many patients have poor perception of their own airflow obstruction and their PEF is a better index of the state of their airways than how they feel.

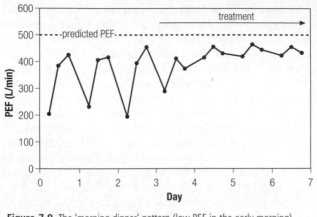

Figure 7.9 The 'morning dipper' pattern (low PEF in the early morning) seen in some asthmatic patients. Note the improvement in the 'dips' with increased anti-inflammatory treatment.

Choosing the appropriate test

It is important to recognise likely clinical situations and to choose the appropriate test for each. For example (see also Chapter 1):

- For patients with respiratory symptoms such as dyspnoea, wheeze, chronic cough and sputum production and exercise intolerance, spirometry is indicated to diagnose and differentiate diseases causing ventilatory abnormality of obstructive or restrictive type.
- In patients with COPD, spirometry is indicated to follow the progression of the disease, response to interventions, and so on.
- For the diagnosis of asthma, spirometry before and after the administration of a bronchodilator, looking for an obstructive pattern with significant improvement, would apply. It is usually necessary to repeat spirometric assessment of airway function at follow-up visits in asthma and other lung conditions where change can occur over short periods of time.

- In patients suspected of having asthma but in whom baseline spirometry is normal, it may be appropriate to confirm the diagnosis by measuring airway reactivity by provocation testing, with measurement of spirometry before and after provocation by exercise or by inhalation of histamine, methacholine or hypertonic saline.
- To identify asthma triggers or treatment responses over long periods of time, regular PEF monitoring by the asthmatic patient is preferred.
- If upper airway obstruction is suspected, flow-volume curve with particular emphasis on inspiration is the best test. It is not recommended to use FEV_1 % predicted to grade obstruction if the cause is upper airway obstruction.
- To assess preoperative risk in the elderly and respiratory compromised, particularly if undergoing abdominal or thoracic surgery, the FEV_1, FVC and FEV_1/FVC ratio are the most useful indices. If an obstructive ventilatory defect is present the anaesthetist would like to know whether there was improvement after the administration of a bronchodilator.
- To assess smoking-related damage at an early stage, evidence of airflow obstruction should be sought systematically using spirometry. This information can be helpful in convincing smokers to give up the habit.
- Serial spirometric measurements are useful to quantify severity and to follow the progression and response to therapy of respiratory diseases such as COPD, asthma and interstitial lung disease.

Here measures such as FEV_1 and FVC may be helpful in asthma but in COPD measurement of IC as an index of hyperinflation also has clinical utility and better correlation with functional outcomes.

An improvement in FEV_1 of $\geq$ 12% and $\geq$ 0.2 L is regarded as a positive bronchodilator response (Pellegrino et al. 2005).

In COPD, FEV_1 by definition does not change with bronchodilators. Here improvement in measures such as IC correlates better with symptoms and functional status. Although detailed studies are needed to better establish the magnitude of a clinically meaningful change, an increase of about 10% in dynamic IC with exercise is considered a clinically significant improvement. Such increases correlate with dyspnoea scores and exercise endurance time as demonstrated in recent Canadian studies, for example O'Donnell 2000.

Summary

Abnormal spirometry is usually classified as an obstructive, restrictive or mixed ventilatory defect. The most commonly seen defect is airflow obstruction, which is characterised by reduced expiratory flows (for example, COPD and current asthma) and usually results in a curvilinear expiratory flow-volume curve. In a restrictive ventilatory defect the patient has no difficulty blowing out quickly but the FVC (and VC) are significantly reduced due to small lungs (for example, pulmonary fibrosis). A mixed ventilatory defect is characterised by both airflow obstruction and small lungs. The shape of the flow-volume loop can be useful diagnostically and can be interpreted at a glance. The degree of reversibility of airflow obstruction following the administration of a bronchodilator is commonly assessed. A significant response is considered to have occurred if the FEV_1 (or FVC) improves by $\geq 12\%$ and $\geq 0.2L$ compared to pre-bronchodilator values. The degree of airway hyperresponsiveness can be assessed by measuring spirometry before and after incremental doses of a bronchoconstricting agent (for example, methacholine) or exercise.

Chapter 8

Case histories

The 10 cases histories in this section illustrate the utility of spirometry in the diagnosis and management of patients with lung disease or respiratory symptoms and in the screening of subjects (for example pre-employment, scuba diving and preoperative screening).

The predicted values are taken from the tables given in Appendix C (pp. 113–33). Both the mean predicted and lower limit of normal (LLN) are given; the latter is used to determine whether a given result is abnormal and the former is used to compute the percent predicted.

Note that the interpretation of spirometry is greatly facilitated when the patient's symptoms (for example, wheezing), smoking history, recent bronchodilator use and the clinical question being asked by the referring physician are known.

Note that in the following cases, the identification of an apparent restrictive defect on spirometry needs to be confirmed and quantified by measuring lung volumes.

Case 1

Case history
- Male of 25 years, height 175 cm
- Never smoked
- No history of respiratory disease
- Normal chest X-ray
- Referred for pre-employment lung function tests

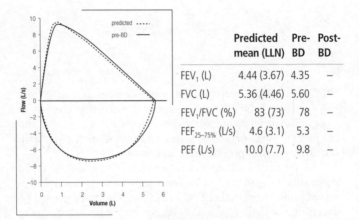

	Predicted mean (LLN)	Pre-BD	Post-BD
FEV_1 (L)	4.44 (3.67)	4.35	–
FVC (L)	5.36 (4.46)	5.60	–
FEV_1/FVC (%)	83 (73)	78	–
$FEF_{25-75\%}$ (L/s)	4.6 (3.1)	5.3	–
PEF (L/s)	10.0 (7.7)	9.8	–

Interpretation: The shape of the flow-volume loop and all spirometric indices are within the normal range, indicating normal ventilatory function. This provides useful baseline lung function data for future comparison.

Case 2

Case history
- Male of 20 years, height 170 cm
- Never smoked
- History of episodic wheeze and chest tightness, particularly in the early morning and during exercise. PEF performed by his family doctor was 43% below the predicted value.
- Referred to confirm diagnosis of asthma and document the degree of reversibility

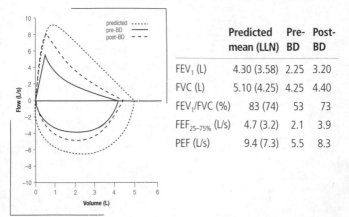

	Predicted mean (LLN)	Pre-BD	Post-BD
FEV_1 (L)	4.30 (3.58)	2.25	3.20
FVC (L)	5.10 (4.25)	4.25	4.40
FEV_1/FVC (%)	83 (74)	53	73
$FEF_{25-75\%}$ (L/s)	4.7 (3.2)	2.1	3.9
PEF (L/s)	9.4 (7.3)	5.5	8.3

Interpretation: The concavity in the expiratory flow-volume curve indicates an obstructive ventilatory defect. Pre-bronchodilator FEV_1/FVC ratio is 53% and FEV_1 is 52% predicted indicating a moderately severe obstructive ventilatory defect. There was a 42% (0.95 L) improvement in FEV_1 post-bronchodilator indicating substantial reversibility.

Pathophysiology: These results are highly suggestive of asthma. In asthma, the airflow obstruction is due to contraction of bronchial smooth muscle (reversible), inflammatory thickening of bronchial mucosa (may improve with steroids) and mucus in the bronchial tubes. Hyperinflation may be present (high TLC and/or FRC) but the diffusing capacity of the lung for carbon monoxide (DLCO) is often normal.

3

ase history
- Male of 73 years, height 165 cm
- Smoker of 50 years (65 pack-years)
- History of increasing shortness of breath, chest infections, chronic cough and hospital admissions (×2 in the past 2 years) for respiratory failure secondary to pneumonia
- Recent chest X-ray shows significant hyperinflation.
- Referred for lung function tests to document ventilatory function and response to bronchodilator

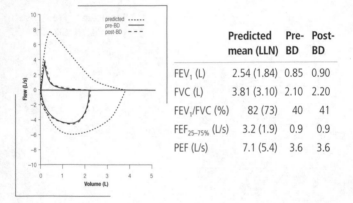

	Predicted mean (LLN)	Pre-BD	Post-BD
FEV$_1$ (L)	2.54 (1.84)	0.85	0.90
FVC (L)	3.81 (3.10)	2.10	2.20
FEV$_1$/FVC (%)	82 (73)	40	41
FEF$_{25-75\%}$ (L/s)	3.2 (1.9)	0.9	0.9
PEF (L/s)	7.1 (5.4)	3.6	3.6

Interpretation: The deep (pressure-dependent) concavity in the expiratory flow-volume curve and low FEV$_1$/FVC ratio and low pre-bronchodilator FEV$_1$ (33% predicted) indicate a very severe obstructive ventilatory defect. There was no significant improvement post-bronchodilator (salbutamol plus ipratropium bromide). With this degree of airflow obstruction the reduced FVC is probably a consequence of airway closure. These results are consistent with severe chronic obstructive pulmonary disease (COPD).

Pathophysiology: In COPD, the airflow obstruction is due to inflammatory thickening and distortion of the airway walls (small airway disease) and to expiratory collapse of airways due to loss of elastic support (emphysema) from the parenchyma. The VC is often well preserved until the disease is severe. In emphysema RV, FRC and TLC are usua[lly] increased, indicating gas trapping (high RV) an[d] hyperinflation (high FRC and/or TLC). The diffusing capacity for carbon monoxide (DLCO) is also reduced.

ase 4

Case history
- Female of 40 years, height 165 cm
- Ex-smoker for 10 years; estimated consumption of 11 pack-years
- No significant history of respiratory disease other than occasional upper respiratory tract infections
- No unusual findings on recent chest X-ray
- Referred for routine lung function tests prior to abdominal surgery

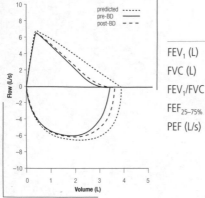

	Predicted mean (LLN)	Pre-BD	Post-BD
FEV$_1$ (L)	3.11 (2.51)	2.59	2.68
FVC (L)	3.81 (3.10)	3.35	3.45
FEV$_1$/FVC (%)	82 (73)	75	77
FEF$_{25-75\%}$ (L/s)	3.2 (1.9)	1.6	1.8
PEF (L/s)	7.1 (5.4)	6.9	6.9

Interpretation: The expiratory flow-volume curve shows abnormally low flows at low lung volumes (and low FEF$_{25-75\%}$) suggesting that the small airways rather than the large airways are abnormally narrow during forced expiration. This is confirmed by the normal FEV$_1$ and PEF but reduced FEF$_{25-75\%}$ (less than the LLN). Post-bronchodilator, there was no significant improvement in FEV$_1$ or small airway function. These results suggest the presence of small airway disease, probably the result of her smoking history.

Case 5

Case history
- Male of 40 years, height 170 cm
- Recent history of waking early in the morning with chest tightness and cough
- The general practitioner advised the patient to purchase a peak flow meter and to monitor his PEF on waking, at noon and before retiring
- After reviewing the results, the physician prescribed salbutamol and inhaled steroids
- The patient then monitored his PEF again

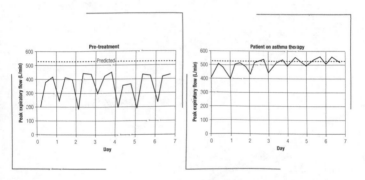

Interpretation: The pre-treatment peak flow chart collected over a 7-day period shows wide swings in PEF (195 to 440 L/min) with the lowest reading occurring in the morning upon waking. During the day, the PEF increased to near the predicted value. These results support the patient's symptoms and are diagnostic of asthma. The general practitioner prescribed salbutamol and inhaled corticosteroids. A further 7 days of self-monitoring showed marked improvement in PEF and the patient's symptoms resolved.

Pathophysiology: These results are highly suggestive of asthma. In asthma, the airflow obstruction is due to contraction of bronchial smooth muscle (reversible), inflammatory thickening of bronchial mucosa and mucus in the bronchial tubes.

Case 6

Case history
- Female of 40 years, height 170 cm
- Non-smoker, no past history of respiratory problems
- 5 years of joint aches and morning stiffness affecting hand, wrist elbows, shoulders and knees
- Recent chest X-ray shows diffuse lung filtrate
- Referred for assessment of dyspnoea

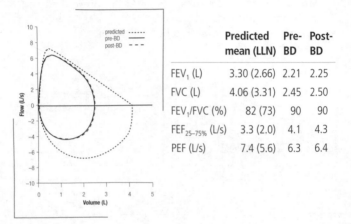

	Predicted mean (LLN)	Pre-BD	Post-BD
FEV_1 (L)	3.30 (2.66)	2.21	2.25
FVC (L)	4.06 (3.31)	2.45	2.50
FEV_1/FVC (%)	82 (73)	90	90
$FEF_{25-75\%}$ (L/s)	3.3 (2.0)	4.1	4.3
PEF (L/s)	7.4 (5.6)	6.3	6.4

Interpretation: The flow-volume loop shows a reduced forced vital capacity and FEV_1 with a well-preserved FEV_1/FVC ratio and maximal flows. This is consistent with a restrictive ventilatory defect. FVC is 60% predicted so this is a moderate restrictive defect. As expected, there is no significant change after bronchodilator.

Pathophysiology: In this patient, the restrictive ventilatory defect was found to be due to fibrosing alveolitis associated with rheumatoid arthritis. The expiratory flows are well preserved relative to her reduced lung volume (her TLC is 67% predicted) due to increased traction on the airways from the stiff parenchymal tissue causing distension of the airways. The static lung volumes (TLC, FRC, RV) are reduced because the overall size of the lungs is restricted by inflammatory and fibrotic scar tissue. The diffusing capacity for carbon monoxide (DLCO) is usually reduced due to inflammation and fibrosis of the alveolar-capillary membrane.

...ase 7

Case history
- Male of 30 years, height 180 cm
- Non-smoker, no past history of respiratory problems
- Presents with 2 years of progressive limb muscle weakness and wasting
- In the past 2 months has noted exertional breathlessness and mild daytime sleepiness
- Recent chest X-ray is normal
- Referred for investigation of his increased breathlessness

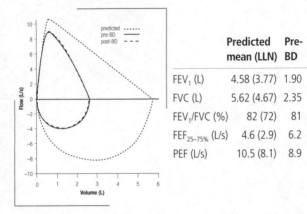

	Predicted mean (LLN)	Pre-BD	Post-BD
FEV_1 (L)	4.58 (3.77)	1.90	1.95
FVC (L)	5.62 (4.67)	2.35	2.35
FEV_1/FVC (%)	82 (72)	81	83
$FEF_{25-75\%}$ (L/s)	4.6 (2.9)	6.2	6.2
PEF (L/s)	10.5 (8.1)	8.9	9.2

Interpretation: The flow-volume loop shows normal expiratory but reduced inspiratory flows consistent with weak inspiratory muscles. The forced vital capacity is markedly reduced (42% predicted), suggesting a severe restrictive ventilatory defect. If the absolute lung volume, rather than expired volume, was plotted on the horizontal axis, then it would be evident that the reduced FVC was a consequence of failure to fully inspire and expire. Further investigation showed that the maximal inspiratory pressure that the patient can generate is only 30 cmH$_2$O and daytime hypercapnoea is present. These results are consistent with diaphragmatic weakness as part of a muscular dystrophy. The nocturnal daytime sleepiness is probably due to sleep fragmentation associated with nocturnal worsening of respiratory failure during sleep. The diffusing capacity for carbon monoxide (DLCO) may be mildly reduced but when expressed per litre of lung volume (DLCO/VA) it is usually significantly elevated with ventilatory restriction in the absence of parenchymal lung disease.

Case 8

Case history
- Male of 65 years, height 179 cm
- Long history of cigarette smoking (50 pack-years)
- Gradually increasing cough, and breathlessness. Sputum has recently been tinged with blood and he has begun to develop stridor
- Recent chest X-ray shows thickening of the mediastinum and right upper lobe mass
- Spirometry is requested pre-bronchoscopy

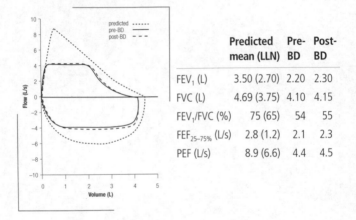

	Predicted mean (LLN)	Pre-BD	Post-BD
FEV$_1$ (L)	3.50 (2.70)	2.20	2.30
FVC (L)	4.69 (3.75)	4.10	4.15
FEV$_1$/FVC (%)	75 (65)	54	55
FEF$_{25-75\%}$ (L/s)	2.8 (1.2)	2.1	2.3
PEF (L/s)	8.9 (6.6)	4.4	4.5

Interpretation: An obstructive ventilatory defect (low FEV$_1$/FVC ratio) with little improvement post-bronchodilator. The flow-volume loop shows a plateau in both expiratory and inspiratory flows (that is, truncation). The forced vital capacity is little affected but it takes a longer time than normal to empty, as indicated by the reduced FEV$_1$/FVC ratio. The shape of the flow-volume loop is characteristic of a rigid large airway obstruction. In this case, the cause is an obstructing carcinoma of the trachea.

Case 9

Case history
- Male of 30 years, height 185 cm
- Injured in a football match with an accidental kick to the throat when knocked down in a crowded pack
- Struggling for breath when carried from the ground by trainers
- Noted to have marked inspiratory stridor and agitation when brought to casualty by ambulance
- Spirometry was performed with difficulty in casualty

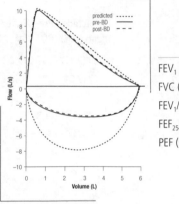

	Predicted mean (LLN)	Pre-BD	Post-BD
FEV_1 (L)	4.83 (3.98)	4.75	4.70
FVC (L)	5.96 (4.96)	5.95	5.80
FEV_1/FVC (%)	82 (72)	80	81
$FEF_{25-75\%}$ (L/s)	4.7 (3.0)	4.5	4.5
PEF (L/s)	10.9 (8.4)	10.7	10.8

Interpretation: The major abnormality in the flow-volume loop is selective truncation of maximal inspiratory flow. This is caused during inspiration by the extra-thoracic upper airway collapsing as it has lost its rigid support and is sucked inward by a negative intra-luminal pressure (that is, sub-atmospheric pressure). The maximal expiratory flow is normal as a positive intra-luminal pressure is developed, causing the upper airway to distend. The shape of this flow-volume loop is typical of a floppy (that is, dynamic) extra-thoracic airway obstruction. In this case, the cause was a fractured larynx.

Case 10

Case history
- Female of 45 years, height 155 cm
- Long history of smoking (35 pack-years)
- Recent history of chest tightness, especially on the left side
- Weight loss is starting to occur
- Chest X-ray is within normal limits
- Spirometry is requested, as is a bronchoscopy

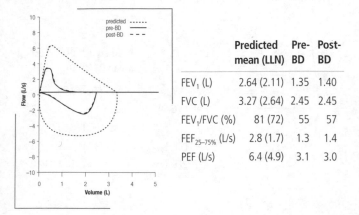

	Predicted mean (LLN)	Pre-BD	Post-BD
FEV$_1$ (L)	2.64 (2.11)	1.35	1.40
FVC (L)	3.27 (2.64)	2.45	2.45
FEV$_1$/FVC (%)	81 (72)	55	57
FEF$_{25–75\%}$ (L/s)	2.8 (1.7)	1.3	1.4
PEF (L/s)	6.4 (4.9)	3.1	3.0

Interpretation: An obstructive ventilatory defect is present (low FEV$_1$ and FEV$_1$/FVC ratio, and curvilinearity in descending limb of the expiratory flow-volume curve) with little reversibility post-bronchodilator. The FEV$_1$ % predicted is 51% indicating that the obstructive defect is moderately severe. The shape of the flow-volume loop is an unusual biconcave with marked flow reduction in the latter parts of both the inspiratory and expiratory curves. This shape is consistent with carcinoma of one of the main bronchi. Since one bronchus is obstructed, air flows at unequal rates from the left and right lungs. In this patient, the right lung empties and fills much faster than the left (obstructed) lung.

Summary

These case histories demonstrate the value of measuring spirometry in clinical practice. The most common abnormalities are intermittent and chronic airflow obstruction characterised by reduced expiratory flows. In addition, serial measurements can be very useful in the management of patients to assess intermittent airways obstruction, disease progression and response to therapy. The cases also illustrate the value of the shape of the flow-volume curve or loop in the interpretation of results. Several of the cases (especially Case 9) illustrate the importance of recording the inspired as well as expired flow volume curve. In Case 9, expiration is normal and the life-threatening abnormality would have been missed using equipment that did not report inspiration. However, the results obtained are of clinical value only if the test is performed using a calibrated spirometer and the patient has been actively coaxed to perform the correct breathing manoeuvre.

PART 4

Chapter 9
Mechanics of breathing

Gas flow through the airways—how airflow is produced

Gas will flow through any tube if the pressure at one end is higher than that at the other. The magnitude of the gas flow will depend largely on the pressure difference between the ends of the tube and the resistance of the tube. The latter has components of frictional resistance between the gas molecules and the side wall of the tube and the energy required to produce convective acceleration of the gas molecules.

In life, the respiratory muscles generate pressure in the pleural space surrounding the lung that, in turn, influences alveolar pressure (the pressure driving gas in and out of the lung). The pressure difference between the alveoli and lips $(P_1 - P_2)$, produces airflow and the magnitude of the airflow depends on the resistance of the airways according to the relationship shown in Figure 9.1.

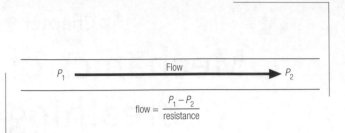

$$flow = \frac{P_1 - P_2}{resistance}$$

Figure 9.1 Factors determining flow of gas through an airway

Tidal breathing

Inspiratory work is performed by the diaphragm and intercostal muscles to generate a negative pressure within the pleural space. This creates a negative alveolar pressure that results in inspiratory airflow. Normally, expiration at rest is a passive process with expiratory flow produced by the potential energy stored in the elastic lung tissue with relaxation of the inspiratory muscles. During quiet breathing in healthy subjects, the pressure in the pleural space (P_{pl}) is about 4 or 5 cmH$_2$O below atmospheric during inspiration and 4 or 5 cmH$_2$O above atmospheric during expiration.

Forced respiratory manoeuvres

The respiratory muscles generate large intra-pleural pressures, and both forced inspiration and forced expiration are active processes. The large pleural pressure creates a much larger pressure difference between the alveoli and lips, thus producing a much greater airflow than during quiet breathing.

Patterns of airflow in the human airways

The human bronchial tree consists of some 26 generations of branching tubes from the single trachea to the very numerous terminal bronchioles. Figure 9.2 shows that the total cross-sectional area of the airways increases greatly from a few square centimetres in the trachea to a total area of about

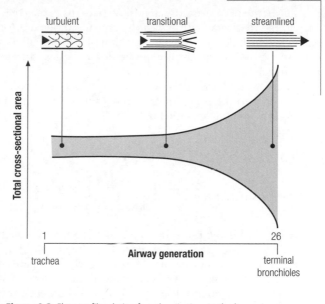

Figure 9.2 Flow profiles during forced expiration. In the large airways where cross-sectional area is small, flow is turbulent. Peripherally where cross-sectional area is large, flow is streamlined (or laminar). In between, particularly at branch points, flow is transitional.

10 000 square centimetres at the level of the last generation of terminal bronchioles.

This means that the speed gas moves through the tracheobronchial tree will vary greatly. In the trachea and main bronchi, the gas velocity will be high (small cross-sectional area) but it will travel very slowly through the peripheral airways (large cross-sectional area).

The large differences in gas velocity affect the pattern of gas flow in different parts of the tracheo-bronchial tree (Figure 9.2). In the peripheral airways where gas velocity is low, a *streamlined* (or laminar) flow pattern is present whereas in the trachea, where gas velocity is relatively high, the flow pattern is turbulent. In the medium-sized airways, the flow pattern is a mixture of streamlined and turbulent and is termed *transitional*.

The relevance of these different flow patterns is that they vary in the efficiency with which the pressure difference (or energy) is expended in producing gas flow. The flow patterns are also affected by the physical properties of the gas (such as gas density).

Under *streamlined* flow conditions, flow is directly proportional to the pressure drop along the airways and is described by Poiseuille's equation:

$$\text{Flow} = (P_1 - P_2) \times \frac{\pi \times r^4}{\mu \times 8 \times L}$$

$$\text{Thus airway resistance} = \frac{(P_1 - P_2)}{\text{Flow}} = \frac{\mu \times 8 \times L}{\pi \times r^4}$$

where $(P_1 - P_2)$ is the pressure drop along the airways when a gas of viscosity μ flows at a given volume rate. L and r are the length and radius of the airway, respectively. This pattern is efficient in terms of pressure expenditure. Note that streamline flow is independent of gas density but is dependent on gas viscosity. Also note that flow and airway resistance are very sensitive to airway radius; if r is doubled, airway resistance decreases 16-fold and if r is halved, $(P_1 - P_2)$ must increase 16-fold if flow is to remain unchanged.

Under *turbulent* conditions, a much higher pressure is required to produce given flow:

$$\text{flow} \propto (P_1 - P_2)^2$$

Thus turbulent flow is inefficient in terms of the pressure drop required to produce a given flow. The density of the gas, as well as its viscosity, affects turbulent flow.

The phenomenon of maximal airflow limitation

One might expect that the harder one tries to breathe, the greater the airflow that can be achieved. While this concept applies during maximal inspiration, it is not true during forced expiration. This is demonstrated by constructing *isovolume pressure-flow curves* (Figure 9.3). These curves

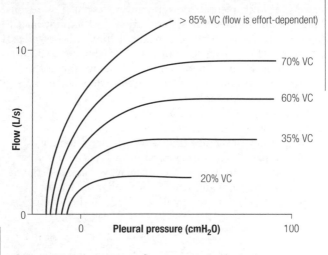

Figure 9.3 Isovolume pressure-flow curve at several lung volumes as a percentage of vital capacity in a normal subject. Expired flow is plotted against pleural pressure. Flow reaches a maximum value at a specific pleural pressure and lung volume; that is, flow does not increase despite increased pleural pressure (effort).

express the relationship between expired flow and pleural pressure (P_{pl}, an index of expiratory effort generated by expiratory muscles) at varying degrees of expiratory effort. The flow corresponding to pleural pressure is plotted for given lung volumes (for example 60%, 70% of the VC). The curve (Figure 9.3) representing near full inspiration (that is, > 85% VC) shows that the maximum expired flow (PEF for this curve) increases with increasing effort (that is, P_{pl}). It demonstrates that PEF remains effort-dependent. At lower lung volumes, expiratory flow increases with effort until a flow maximum is reached. Any further increase in effort does not result in further increases in expiratory flow (flow is effort-independent). Here any increase in expiratory effort is offset by an increase in airway resistance due to greater airway compression.

Thus, at high lung volumes maximal expiratory flow becomes independent of effort. This can be seen more easily if we plot both pleural pressure and maximal flow against lung volume during forced inspiration and expiration (see Figure 9.4). As you can see, maximal flow follows pleural pressure (P_{pl}) during inspiration, but during expiration maximal flow falls off independent of pleural pressure.

Maximal inspiratory flow is effort-dependent and is determined by three factors:

1. the effort applied by the patient
2. the strength of the inspiratory muscles
3. the patency of the upper airways which are under a compressive force during inspiration (that is, sub-atmospheric pressure inside the airway and atmospheric pressure outside) and will tend to collapse. These airways are supported by the cartilage in the wall of the

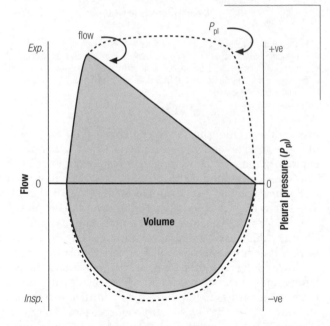

Figure 9.4 Plot of both pleural pressure and maximal flow against volume. Note how the maximal flow follows the degree of effort (P_{pl}) during inspiration but is independent of it during expiration.

trachea and the larynx, and the rigidity of these structures is important in maintaining inspiratory flow. There is also an increase in tone in the dilator muscles of the larynx and pharynx, for example genioglossus and tensor palatini for the pharynx and the posterior cricopharyngeus cricoarytenoid muscles of the larynx (abductors of vocal folds), just preceding and during inspiration, again stabilising these parts of the upper airway against inspiratory collapse.

A number of theories attempt to explain why maximal expiratory flow is effort-independent. These theories include (1) the equal pressure point, (2) flow-limiting segments developing within the airways and (3) wave speed theory. These will be outlined briefly as we explore the forces and mechanisms limiting maximal expiratory flow through the airways.

Theories of airflow obstruction

The equal pressure point

Imagine if we were to take a snapshot at a particular lung volume during forced expiration and analyse the forces producing expiratory flow (see Figure 9.5). Recall that gas

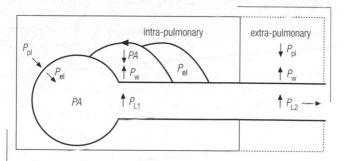

Figure 9.5 Intra-thoracic forces acting on the extra-pulmonary and intra-pulmonary airways. P_{pl} = pleural pressure; P_{el} = elastic recoil pressure; PA = alveolar pressure; P_w = elasticity of the airway wall; P_L = intra-luminal pressure.

flow from the lung is driven by the pressure difference between the alveoli and the mouth. This pressure difference is dissipated in producing flow so that the pressure at any point inside the airway will be somewhere between alveolar and mouth pressure and will be a distending force during forced expiration.

The intra-pulmonary airways are surrounded by alveolar pressure, which pushes inwards, but they are supported by the elastic recoil of the parenchyma maintained through structural attachments extending to the intra-pulmonary airways and by their own airway wall elasticity (P_w). The pressure acting on the outside wall of the airway (extra-luminal pressure) is equal to $PA - P_{el}$ (see Figure 9.5) which we know from analysis of forces on the surface of the lung approximates P_{pl}. Thus, at any instant during expiration the pressure within the alveoli will equal the pleural pressure plus the recoil pressure of the lung (alveolar pressure = $P_{pl} + P_{el}$).

A number of animal studies where the pressure outside the extra-pulmonary airways has been measured during forced expiration have confirmed that this pressure is close to pleural pressure. The pressure across the airway wall (the transmural pressure) will depend on the balance of the pressure outside (pleural pressure) and that inside. Recall that at any point along the airway the pressure will be somewhere between that in the alveoli and at the lips.

The term 'equal pressure point' (EPP) is applied to any point along the airway where the pressure inside the airway equals that outside. Upstream (towards the alveoli during expiration) of the EPP, transmural pressure (P_{tm}) is positive and the airway is distended. However, downstream of the EPP (towards the mouth during expiration) the airway is being compressed because pleural pressure is greater than the pressure within the airway and the elasticity of the airway wall ($P_{pl} > P_{aw}$ and P_{tm} is negative). Because flow is in series, it is possible to describe the maximal expiratory flow (V_{max}) by analysis of the forces in the airway segment upstream from the EPP (R_{us}, resistance of the segment between EPP and alveoli). The driving pressure causing flow (V_{max}) through this segment is the elastic recoil pressure (P_{el}). Thus in the upstream segment:

$$V_{max} = \frac{P_{el}}{R_{us}}$$

Note that the magnitude of the pleural pressure (P_{pl}) does not figure in this equation. Thus, V_{max} depends on the elastic recoil force distending the airways (P_{el}) and the resistance of the airways (R_{us}) and not on pleural pressure (the expiratory effort being generated by the respiratory muscles). Thus, in the downstream segment (between the EPP and mouth):

$$V_{max} = \frac{P_{pl}}{R_{us}}$$

Compression of the airways downstream from the EPP results from greater P_{pl} (that is, effort) making downstream events more difficult to quantify. However, flow through the upstream segment depends on the static recoil pressure (a fixed property of the lung parenchyma) and the distance of the upstream segment of the airways which is under distending force and has more constant geometry. It is thus more convenient to describe V_{max} in terms of its upstream components.

Flow-limiting segment
An extension of the EPP theory was put forward by Pride and colleagues in 1967. This group analysed the transmural pressure gradient (P_{tm}) along the airways; this led them to conclude that pleural pressure outside the airways downstream of EPP would exceed the pressure within the collapsible airways by a sufficient amount to narrow it 'critically'. This causes flow limitation over a segment of the collapsed downstream airway known as the *flow-limiting segment*. The compliance or elasticity of the downstream airway wall in affecting flow limitation is emphasised in this analysis which incorporates the equal pressure point concept outlined earlier.

Wave-speed theory
During expiration, pressure waves are propagated in the airway walls from the interaction between the radial recoil

force of the elastic walls and the axial inertia of the intra-luminal air. The speed of these waves is $(Y\rho)^{0.5}$ where Y (the elastic modulus) is the reciprocal of the specific compliance or distensibility of the airway cross-section and ρ is the density of the gas in the lumen. When airflow through the airway lumen reaches the speed of the pressure wave in the airway wall, flow disturbance causing energy loss prevents any further increase in velocity and a choke point develops at which flow limitation is present.

The flow rate at *wave speed* (V_{ws}) depends on the cross-sectional area, A, the elasticity of the airway wall ($\delta P_{tm}/\delta A$) and the density ρ of the gas. The maximal flow through the airway is then the product of the speed of these waves and the airway cross-section.

Wave speed through uncompressed airways is high, but downstream of the equal pressure points a point is reached where the local wave speed reaches a maximal gas velocity and flow limitation occurs. This is referred to as the choke point.

In summary, all these theories are directly applicable and may work in concert during breathing in humans. The current state of our knowledge is that the mechanical properties of the airways (EPP and flow-limiting segment) are responsible for determining V_{max} at low lung volumes. But for high and mid lung volumes, maximal gas velocity will reach wave speed and flow limitation in large bronchi will occur due to the wave speed rather than effort-related mechanisms. In normal humans, peak expiratory flow during forced expiration occurs very quickly after 25% to 30% of the vital capacity has been expired. Beyond this point, V_{max} becomes independent of effort, provided a certain amount of effort is used. Flow may be then thought of as being determined by:

- elastic recoil pressure of the lung
- flow resistance of the airways between the alveoli and EPP, and
- compliance of the airway wall at choke points.

Consequently, the shape of the maximal expiratory flow-volume curve will depend on changes in either elastic recoil or upstream resistance with volume.

How pulmonary disease affects airflow

From the above discussion we have seen how *expiratory flow* is largely independent of effort and relates to the lung elastic recoil pressure, which decreases linearly with lung volume and the resistance of the upstream airways. Maximal *inspiratory flow* on the other hand will depend on the respiratory effort generated, the inspiratory muscle strength and the calibre of the extra-thoracic airway. Disease of the respiratory system influences maximal airflow via a number of mechanisms.

The expired V_{max} will be reduced because of diminished lung elastic recoil in emphysema. However, in asthma and in small airways disease induced by smoking, air pollution and so on, V_{max} will be decreased largely due to increased R_{us} caused by airway wall thickening and narrowing. On the other hand, V_{max} will be well preserved or even increased in interstitial lung disease (for example, pulmonary fibrosis) where the elastic recoil of the lung tissue is increased and the airways are held wide open by greater than normal elastic recoil forces.

Maximal inspiratory flow is dependent on pleural pressure and airways resistance. Inspiratory flow is thus reduced in asthma and in small airways disease because of the high airways resistance, but is relatively well preserved in emphysema because the airways are distended during inspiration (normal inspiratory airway resistance).

Extra-thoracic airway obstruction (for example, fractured larynx) is particularly likely to limit inspiratory flow because of compression of the upper airway generated by atmospheric pressure (outside) and low pressure inside the upper airway. Diaphragm weakness limits inspiratory flow through the reduced effort achievable (low P_{pl}). Lack of effort when performing spirometry will also reduce inspiratory flow by the same mechanism.

The above abnormalities result in particular shapes of the flow-volume curves. An understanding of the mechanisms of flow limitation outlined above makes recognition of these specific flow-volume curve shape patterns for specific disease processes a meaningful, rational and reliable diagnostic tool.

Summary

Some understanding of the mechanisms of flow limitation greatly assists in the interpretation of spirometry, including the shape of the flow-volume loop. The maximal flow achieved during most of the expiration process is effort-dependent because it is determined by the lung's elastic recoil pressure, resistance of the airways between the alveoli and the equal pressure point, and the compliance of the airways at the choke points. During the entire inspiration, maximal flows are effort-dependent.

Chapter 10
Summary

Measurements of ventilatory function should be part of the routine assessment of patients with respiratory disease. Spirometry affords clinical practice a simple, achievable, evidence-based and critical opportunity to assess the respiratory health of all who cross its doorstep. It similarly affords the community health practitioner the opportunity to assess the respiratory health of the broader general population. Patient self-monitoring with a peak flow meter or similar device is now an accepted part of the day-to-day management of asthma. Spirometry measurements performed in the lung function laboratory, general practitioner's surgery or respiratory specialist's office can detect and quantify respiratory abnormalities and help to differentiate the various disease processes which result in ventilatory impairment. They also have an important role in following the natural history of respiratory disease and its treatment.

Further, spirometry now has an established place in public health practice as a simple and reliable screening tool for detecting respiratory disease, often before it becomes clinically obvious. The high burden of respiratory disease in the developed world where its roots lie in cigarette smoking, atmospheric pollution and an increasing array of occupational and environmental hazards demands detection and management strategies. People at even higher risk are those in developing countries when indoor combustion practices for cooking and heating remain widespread. Furthermore, spirometry has the capacity to detect airway dysfunction long before symptoms develop, bringing the opportunity to remove harmful exposures before disability develops or becomes severe. These factors render spirometry a critically useful investigation in the detection, management and prevention of respiratory disease.

Equipment standards and validation procedures

Equipment standards

Those interested in more detailed knowledge of equipment standards and validation procedures are referred to the standardisation document published jointly by the American Thoracic Society and European Respiratory Society (Miller et al. 2005b). This document describes the minimum recommendations for all spirometers (Table A.1), including monitoring devices, and provides guidelines for their calibration and quality control and gives details of test procedures.

	Table A.1				Minimum Performance Recommendations for Spirometers (Miller et al. 2005b)

Test	Range/accuracy (BTPS)	Time (s)	Flow range (L/s)	Test signal
VC	0.5 to 8.0 L ±3% of reading or ±0.050 L*	30	0–14	3 L syringe
FVC	0.5 to 8.0 L ±3% of reading or ±0.050 L*	15	0–14	24 ATS waveforms (1994); 3 L syringe
FEV_1	0.5 to 8.0 L ±3% of reading or ±0.050 L*	1	0–14	24 ATS waveforms (1994)
Zero time	All timed volumes from a time point determined by back-extrapolation	–	–	Back-extrapolation
PEF	Accuracy: ±10% of reading or ±0.3 L/s* Repeatability: ±5% of reading or ±0.15 L/s*	–	0–14	26 ATS flow waveforms (1994)
$FEF_{25–75\%}$	7 L/s ±5% of reading or ±0.2 L/s*	15	±14	24 ATS waveforms (1994)
Flow	±14 L/s ±5% of reading or ±0.2 L/s*	15	0–14	Manufacturer's proof

Note: Resistance of entire breathing circuit (including barrier filter, if included) should be less than 1.5 cm $H_2O/L/s$ over the flow range 0 to 14 L/s for all indices other than PEF. For PEF the resistance at 200, 400 and 600 L/min should be less than 2.5 cm$H_2O/L/s$.

* Whichever is greater

Validation procedures

The ERS/ATS also describes *validation procedures* to assess the accuracy and reproducibility of both volume-displacement and flow spirometers. This requires the use of an expensive computer-controlled syringe which can produce a variety of expiratory FVC curves with accurately known values for FVC, FEV_1, $FEF_{25-75\%}$ and PEF. Validation is normally carried out by the manufacturer (or an independent testing laboratory) and it is important for prospective purchasers to ensure that the spirometer meets the ERS/ATS criteria and that clear documentation of this is provided.

Correction of volume and flow to BTPS

For most instruments, manual correction of measured volume and flow rates to body temperature and pressure saturated (BTPS) is usually necessary when these are calculated from conventional spirograms, as the expired gas contracts due to gas cooling and the condensation of water vapour (Figure B.1). The appropriate correction factor to apply depends on the temperature and

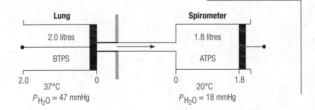

When we blow into a 'cold' spirometer, the volume recorded by the spirometer is less than that displaced from the lungs, due to:
1. gas shrinkage
2. condensation of water vapour (vapour pressure falls)

Figure B.1 Respired volumes (for example FEV_1, FVC) and flows (for example $FEF_{25-75\%}$) are always corrected to body conditions (BTPS—37°C, fully saturated with water vapour). In this schematic, 2.0 litres are emptied from the lung (BTPS) but only 1.8 litres are recorded by the spirometer (ATPS—ambient temperature and pressure saturated).

to a lesser extent on the pressure of the gas as it enters the spirometer or flows through the sensor. This correction assumes that expired air cools instantly as it enters the spirometer.

Computerised spirometers will usually automatically correct to BTPS but the operator will need to specify ambient temperature and barometric pressure unless these are measured directly by the instrument.

Heated pneumotachographs partially overcome the need for the temperature correction by reheating expired gas to a temperature close to that of the body, but some further correction may still be required as the gas will have lost water vapour and will not be fully saturated.

The equation for correcting volumes and flow (for example FEV_1, $FEF_{25-75\%}$, VC, FVC and PEF) from ATPS (atmospheric temperature and pressure, saturated) to BTPS (assuming expired gas cools instantly to spirometer temperature) is:

$$\text{volume (BTPS)} = \text{volume (ATPS)} \times \frac{P_b - H_2O_t}{P_b - 47} \times \frac{310}{273 + t}$$

where volume (ATPS) = volume measured from spirometer chart

P_b = barometric pressure (mmHg)

H_2O_t = saturated water vapour pressure (mmHg) at spirometer temperature, t —see Table B.1

t = spirometry temperature (usually equal to room temperature) in degrees Celsius

47 = saturated water vapour pressure (mmHg) at 37°C

Note that the sensors used in flow spirometers (for example, pneumotachographs) are generally held close to the mouth, so expired gas will not have cooled fully before passing from the lung to the sensor or from the room to the lung. For this and other reasons (for example, some sensors are heated) the ATPS to BTPS correction equation above may not be appropriate. Under these circumstances, the correct factor should have been determined by the manufacturer and is usually applied automatically, and may also include the

effect of temperature and gas composition on the viscosity
and density of expired air.

Table B.1 lists the appropriate corrections over the
temperature range 17°C to 32°C assuming the expired gas
entering the spirometer is fully saturated and that the
barometric pressure is 760 mmHg. The correction factors
assume that expired gas cools instantly to spirometer
temperature. (Note: at sea level, day-to-day variations in
barometric pressure do not significantly affect the magnitude
of the BTPS correction factor (Johns et al. 2004).

Table B.1	Conversion factors from ATPS to BTPS	
Spirometer temperature (Celsius)	Saturated water vapour (mmHg)	BTPS factor
17	14.5	1.118
18	15.5	1.113
19	16.5	1.108
20	17.5	1.102
21	18.7	1.096
22	19.8	1.091
23	21.1	1.085
24	22.4	1.080
25	23.8	1.075
26	25.2	1.069
27	26.7	1.063
28	28.3	1.057
29	30.0	1.051
30	31.8	1.045
31	33.7	1.039
32	35.7	1.032

Assumes a barometric pressure of 760 mmHg

Predicted normal values

The use of a fixed percent of predicted (for example, 80%) to define the lower limit of normal is widespread despite being shown to be statistically invalid. A more appropriate approach is based on the use of the residual standard deviation (RSD) from regression analyses (usually multiple variables are regressed, that is, age and height) but this is only possible if the survey population data are normally distributed for subjects of all ages and heights. This is because most predicted normal data is homoscedastic, that is, variation in these parameters is uniform across the age and height ranges. The addition or subtraction of 1.64 times the RSD from the mean predicted value results in an upper (or lower, but not both) limit of normality with a confidence level such that 95% of the subjects in the survey lie above the lower limit.

Mean predicted normal values and lower limit of normal

Mean predicted and lower limit of normal (LLN) of Caucasian males and females between 8 and 80 years of age for the major expiratory indices are given in the following tables (Hankinson, Odencrantz & Fedan 1999 and Hankinson, Crapo & Jensen 2003). Age is in years; height in centimetres.

Table C.1

Predicted normal values: mean and lower limit of normal (Hankinson, Odencrantz & Fedan 1999)

FVC (L) Male

Age (yrs)	20 Mean	20 LLN	25 Mean	25 LLN	30 Mean	30 LLN	35 Mean	35 LLN	40 Mean	40 LLN	45 Mean	45 LLN	50 Mean	50 LLN	55 Mean	55 LLN	60 Mean	60 LLN	65 Mean	65 LLN	70 Mean	70 LLN	75 Mean	75 LLN	80 Mean	80 LLN
145 cm	3.63	3.01	3.57	2.95	3.50	2.88	3.42	2.80	3.32	2.70	3.21	2.59	3.09	2.47	2.95	2.33	2.80	2.18	2.63	2.01	2.45	1.83	2.26	1.64	2.06	1.44
150 cm	3.91	3.24	3.85	3.19	3.78	3.12	3.69	3.03	3.60	2.93	3.49	2.82	3.36	2.70	3.22	2.56	3.07	2.41	2.91	2.24	2.73	2.06	2.54	1.87	2.33	1.67
155 cm	4.19	3.48	4.13	3.43	4.06	3.35	3.98	3.27	3.88	3.17	3.77	3.06	3.64	2.94	3.51	2.80	3.36	2.65	3.19	2.48	3.01	2.30	2.82	2.11	2.62	1.91
160 cm	4.48	3.73	4.43	3.67	4.36	3.60	4.27	3.52	4.17	3.42	4.06	3.31	3.94	3.18	3.80	3.05	3.65	2.89	3.48	2.73	3.31	2.55	3.11	2.36	2.91	2.15
165 cm	4.79	3.98	4.73	3.93	4.66	3.86	4.57	3.77	4.48	3.67	4.37	3.56	4.24	3.44	4.10	3.30	3.95	3.15	3.79	2.98	3.61	2.81	3.42	2.61	3.21	2.41
170 cm	5.10	4.25	5.04	4.19	4.97	4.12	4.89	4.04	4.79	3.94	4.68	3.83	4.55	3.70	4.42	3.56	4.26	3.41	4.10	3.25	3.92	3.07	3.73	2.88	3.52	2.67
175 cm	5.42	4.52	5.36	4.46	5.29	4.39	5.21	4.31	5.11	4.21	5.00	4.10	4.88	3.97	4.74	3.83	4.59	3.68	4.42	3.52	4.24	3.34	4.05	3.15	3.85	2.94
180 cm	5.75	4.80	5.69	4.74	5.62	4.67	5.54	4.58	5.44	4.49	5.33	4.38	5.21	4.25	5.07	4.11	4.92	3.96	4.75	3.80	4.57	3.62	4.38	3.43	4.18	3.22
185 cm	6.09	5.08	6.03	5.03	5.96	4.96	5.88	4.87	5.78	4.77	5.67	4.66	5.55	4.54	5.41	4.40	5.26	4.25	5.09	4.08	4.91	3.91	4.72	3.71	4.52	3.51
190 cm	6.44	5.38	6.38	5.32	6.31	5.25	6.23	5.17	6.13	5.07	6.02	4.96	5.90	4.83	5.76	4.69	5.61	4.54	5.44	4.38	5.26	4.20	5.07	4.01	4.87	3.80
195 cm	6.80	5.68	6.74	5.62	6.67	5.55	6.59	5.47	6.49	5.37	6.38	5.26	6.25	5.13	6.12	5.00	5.97	4.84	5.80	4.68	5.62	4.50	5.43	4.31	5.22	4.10

Table C.1 continued
(Hankinson, Odencrantz & Fedan 1999)

FEV$_1$ (L) Male

Age (yrs)	20		25		30		35		40		45		50		55		60		65		70		75		80	
	Mean	LLN	Mean	LLN	Mean	LLN	Mean	LLN	Mean	LLN	Mean	LLN	Mean	LLN	Mean	LLN	Mean	LLN	Mean	LLN	Mean	LLN	Mean	LLN	Mean	LLN
145 cm	3.19	2.66	3.08	2.56	2.97	2.45	2.85	2.33	2.72	2.20	2.58	2.06	2.44	1.91	2.28	1.76	2.12	1.59	1.94	1.42	1.76	1.24	1.57	1.05	1.37	0.85
150 cm	3.40	2.84	3.29	2.73	3.18	2.62	3.06	2.50	2.93	2.37	2.79	2.23	2.64	2.08	2.49	1.93	2.32	1.76	2.15	1.59	1.97	1.41	1.78	1.22	1.58	1.02
155 cm	3.61	3.01	3.51	2.91	3.39	2.80	3.27	2.68	3.14	2.55	3.01	2.41	2.86	2.26	2.70	2.11	2.54	1.94	2.37	1.77	2.19	1.59	2.00	1.40	1.80	1.20
160 cm	3.83	3.20	3.73	3.09	3.62	2.98	3.50	2.86	3.37	2.73	3.23	2.59	3.08	2.44	2.93	2.29	2.76	2.12	2.59	1.95	2.41	1.77	2.22	1.58	2.02	1.38
165 cm	4.06	3.38	3.96	3.28	3.85	3.17	3.73	3.05	3.60	2.92	3.46	2.78	3.31	2.63	3.15	2.48	2.99	2.31	2.82	2.14	2.64	1.96	2.45	1.77	2.25	1.57
170 cm	4.30	3.58	4.19	3.47	4.08	3.36	3.96	3.24	3.83	3.11	3.69	2.97	3.55	2.83	3.39	2.67	3.23	2.51	3.05	2.33	2.87	2.15	2.68	1.96	2.48	1.76
175 cm	4.54	3.78	4.44	3.67	4.33	3.56	4.20	3.44	4.07	3.31	3.94	3.17	3.79	3.03	3.63	2.87	3.47	2.71	3.30	2.53	3.12	2.35	2.93	2.16	2.73	1.97
180 cm	4.79	3.98	4.69	3.88	4.58	3.77	4.45	3.65	4.32	3.52	4.19	3.38	4.04	3.23	3.88	3.08	3.72	2.91	3.55	2.74	3.37	2.56	3.18	2.37	2.98	2.17
185 cm	5.05	4.20	4.95	4.09	4.83	3.98	4.71	3.86	4.58	3.73	4.44	3.59	4.30	3.44	4.14	3.29	3.98	3.13	3.80	2.95	3.62	2.77	3.43	2.58	3.24	2.38
190 cm	5.31	4.41	5.21	4.31	5.10	4.20	4.98	4.08	4.85	3.95	4.71	3.81	4.56	3.66	4.41	3.51	4.24	3.34	4.07	3.17	3.89	2.99	3.70	2.80	3.50	2.60
195 cm	5.58	4.64	5.48	4.53	5.37	4.42	5.25	4.30	5.12	4.17	4.98	4.03	4.83	3.89	4.68	3.73	4.51	3.57	4.34	3.39	4.16	3.21	3.97	3.02	3.77	2.82

Table C.1 continued
(Hankinson, Odencrantz & Fedan 1999)

FEV$_1$/FVC (%) Male

Age (yrs)	20		25		30		35		40		45		50		55		60		65		70		75		80	
	Mean	LLN	Mean	LLN	Mean	LLN	Mean	LLN	Mean	LLN	Mean	LLN	Mean	LLN	Mean	LLN	Mean	LLN	Mean	LLN	Mean	LLN	Mean	LLN	Mean	LLN
All heights	83.9	74.3	82.9	73.2	81.9	72.2	80.8	71.2	79.8	70.1	78.8	69.1	77.7	68.1	76.7	67.0	75.7	66.0	74.6	65.0	73.6	63.9	72.6	62.9	71.5	61.9

Table C.1 continued
(Hankinson, Odencrantz & Fedan 1999)

$FEF_{25-75\%}$ (L/sec) Male

Age (yrs)	20		25		30		35		40		45		50		55		60		65		70		75		80	
	Mean	LLN	Mean	LLN	Mean	LLN	Mean	LLN	Mean	LLN	Mean	LLN	Mean	LLN	Mean	LLN	Mean	LLN	Mean	LLN	Mean	LLN	Mean	LLN	Mean	LLN
145 cm	3.88	2.81	3.63	2.56	3.38	2.32	3.13	2.07	2.88	1.82	2.63	1.57	2.38	1.32	2.13	1.07	1.88	0.82	1.63	0.57	1.38	0.32	1.13	0.07	0.88	–
150 cm	4.03	2.89	3.78	2.64	3.53	2.39	3.28	2.14	3.03	1.89	2.78	1.64	2.53	1.39	2.28	1.14	2.03	0.89	1.78	0.65	1.53	0.40	1.28	0.15	1.03	–
155 cm	4.19	2.97	3.94	2.72	3.69	2.47	3.44	2.22	3.19	1.97	2.94	1.72	2.69	1.47	2.44	1.23	2.19	0.98	1.94	0.73	1.69	0.48	1.44	0.23	1.19	–
160 cm	4.35	3.06	4.10	2.81	3.85	2.56	3.60	2.31	3.35	2.06	3.10	1.81	2.85	1.56	2.60	1.31	2.35	1.06	2.10	0.81	1.85	0.56	1.60	0.31	1.35	0.06
165 cm	4.52	3.14	4.27	2.89	4.02	2.64	3.77	2.39	3.52	2.14	3.27	1.89	3.02	1.64	2.77	1.39	2.52	1.14	2.27	0.90	2.02	0.65	1.77	0.40	1.52	0.15
170 cm	4.69	3.23	4.44	2.98	4.19	2.73	3.94	2.48	3.69	2.23	3.44	1.98	3.19	1.73	2.94	1.48	2.69	1.23	2.44	0.98	2.19	0.73	1.94	0.48	1.69	0.23
175 cm	4.87	3.32	4.62	3.07	4.37	2.82	4.12	2.57	3.87	2.32	3.62	2.07	3.37	1.82	3.12	1.57	2.87	1.32	2.62	1.08	2.37	0.83	2.12	0.58	1.87	0.33
180 cm	5.05	3.42	4.80	3.17	4.55	2.92	4.30	2.67	4.05	2.42	3.80	2.17	3.55	1.92	3.31	1.67	3.06	1.42	2.81	1.17	2.56	0.92	2.31	0.67	2.06	0.42
185 cm	5.24	3.51	4.99	3.26	4.74	3.01	4.49	2.76	4.24	2.51	3.99	2.26	3.74	2.01	3.49	1.77	3.24	1.52	2.99	1.27	2.74	1.02	2.49	0.77	2.25	0.52
190 cm	5.44	3.61	5.19	3.36	4.94	3.11	4.69	2.86	4.44	2.61	4.19	2.36	3.94	2.11	3.69	1.86	3.44	1.61	3.19	1.36	2.94	1.12	2.69	0.87	2.44	0.62
195 cm	5.64	3.71	5.39	3.46	5.14	3.22	4.89	2.97	4.64	2.72	4.39	2.47	4.14	2.22	3.89	1.97	3.64	1.72	3.39	1.47	3.14	1.22	2.89	0.97	2.64	0.72

Table C.1 continued
(Hankinson, Odencrantz & Fedan 1999)

PEF (L/min) Male

Age (yrs)	20 Mean	20 LLN	25 Mean	25 LLN	30 Mean	30 LLN	35 Mean	35 LLN	40 Mean	40 LLN	45 Mean	45 LLN	50 Mean	50 LLN	55 Mean	55 LLN	60 Mean	60 LLN	65 Mean	65 LLN	70 Mean	70 LLN	75 Mean	75 LLN	80 Mean	80 LLN
145 cm	446	354	453	361	457	364	456	364	452	359	443	351	431	339	415	322	395	302	371	278	343	251	311	219	276	183
150 cm	468	369	475	377	479	380	478	379	474	375	465	366	453	354	437	338	417	318	393	294	365	266	333	234	298	199
155 cm	491	385	498	393	502	396	501	395	497	391	488	383	476	370	460	354	440	334	416	310	388	282	356	250	320	215
160 cm	515	402	522	409	525	413	525	412	520	408	512	399	500	387	483	371	463	351	439	327	411	299	380	267	344	231
165 cm	539	419	546	426	550	430	549	429	545	425	536	416	524	404	508	388	488	368	464	344	436	316	404	284	368	249
170 cm	564	437	571	444	575	448	574	447	570	443	561	434	549	422	533	406	513	386	489	362	461	334	429	302	393	266
175 cm	590	455	597	462	600	466	600	465	595	461	587	452	575	440	559	424	539	404	515	380	487	352	455	320	419	285
180 cm	616	474	624	481	627	485	626	484	622	480	614	471	601	459	585	443	565	423	541	399	513	371	482	339	446	303
185 cm	644	493	651	501	654	504	654	503	649	499	641	491	629	478	613	462	593	442	569	418	541	390	509	358	473	323
190 cm	672	513	679	520	682	524	682	523	677	519	669	510	657	498	641	482	621	462	597	438	569	410	537	378	501	343
195 cm	701	534	708	541	711	544	711	544	706	539	698	531	686	518	669	502	649	482	625	458	598	430	566	399	530	363

Table C.1 continued
(Hankinson, Crapo & Jensen 2003)

FVC$_6$ (L) Male

Age (yrs)	20		25		30		35		40		45		50		55		60		65		70		75		80	
	Mean	LLN	Mean	LLN	Mean	LLN	Mean	LLN	Mean	LLN	Mean	LLN	Mean	LLN	Mean	LLN	Mean	LLN	Mean	LLN	Mean	LLN	Mean	LLN	Mean	LLN
145 cm	3.67	3.06	3.58	2.97	3.48	2.87	3.37	2.76	3.24	2.64	3.10	2.50	2.96	2.35	2.80	2.19	2.63	2.02	2.44	1.84	2.25	1.64	2.04	1.44	1.82	1.22
150 cm	3.94	3.29	3.85	3.20	3.75	3.10	3.63	2.99	3.51	2.86	3.37	2.72	3.23	2.58	3.07	2.42	2.89	2.25	2.71	2.06	2.52	1.87	2.31	1.66	2.09	1.44
155 cm	4.21	3.52	4.12	3.43	4.02	3.33	3.91	3.22	3.79	3.09	3.65	2.96	3.50	2.81	3.34	2.65	3.17	2.48	2.99	2.30	2.79	2.10	2.59	1.90	2.37	1.68
160 cm	4.50	3.76	4.41	3.67	4.31	3.57	4.20	3.46	4.07	3.33	3.94	3.20	3.79	3.05	3.63	2.89	3.45	2.72	3.27	2.54	3.08	2.34	2.87	2.14	2.66	1.92
165 cm	4.80	4.01	4.71	3.92	4.60	3.82	4.49	3.71	4.37	3.58	4.23	3.45	4.08	3.30	3.92	3.14	3.75	2.97	3.57	2.79	3.38	2.59	3.17	2.38	2.95	2.17
170 cm	5.10	4.27	5.01	4.18	4.91	4.08	4.80	3.96	4.67	3.84	4.54	3.70	4.39	3.56	4.23	3.40	4.06	3.22	3.87	3.04	3.68	2.85	3.47	2.64	3.26	2.42
175 cm	5.41	4.53	5.32	4.44	5.22	4.34	5.11	4.23	4.99	4.10	4.85	3.97	4.70	3.82	4.54	3.66	4.37	3.49	4.19	3.31	3.99	3.11	3.79	2.90	3.57	2.69
180 cm	5.74	4.80	5.65	4.71	5.55	4.61	5.43	4.50	5.31	4.37	5.17	4.24	5.02	4.09	4.86	3.93	4.69	3.76	4.51	3.58	4.32	3.38	4.11	3.18	3.89	2.96
185 cm	6.07	5.08	5.98	4.99	5.88	4.89	5.76	4.78	5.64	4.65	5.50	4.52	5.36	4.37	5.20	4.21	5.02	4.04	4.84	3.86	4.65	3.66	4.44	3.45	4.22	3.24
190 cm	6.41	5.37	6.32	5.28	6.22	5.18	6.10	5.06	5.98	4.94	5.84	4.80	5.70	4.66	5.54	4.50	5.37	4.33	5.18	4.14	4.99	3.95	4.78	3.74	4.56	3.52
195 cm	6.76	5.66	6.67	5.57	6.57	5.47	6.45	5.36	6.33	5.23	6.19	5.10	6.05	4.95	5.89	4.79	5.72	4.62	5.53	4.44	5.34	4.24	5.13	4.04	4.91	3.82

Table C.1 continued
(Hankinson, Crapo & Jensen 2003)

FEV$_1$/FVC$_6$ (%) Male

Age (yrs)	20		25		30		35		40		45		50		55		60		65		70		75		80	
	Mean	LLN	Mean	LLN	Mean	LLN	Mean	LLN	Mean	LLN	Mean	LLN	Mean	LLN	Mean	LLN	Mean	LLN	Mean	LLN	Mean	LLN	Mean	LLN	Mean	LLN
All heights	84.5	75.5	83.8	74.8	83.2	74.2	82.5	73.5	81.8	72.8	81.1	72.1	80.4	71.4	79.7	70.7	79.1	70.0	78.4	69.4	77.7	68.7	77.0	68.0	76.3	67.3

Table C.1 continued
(Hankinson, Crapo & Jensen 2003)

FEF$_{25-75\%}$ (L/sec) Male

Age (yrs)	20		25		30		35		40		45		50		55		60		65		70		75		80	
	Mean	LLN	Mean	LLN	Mean	LLN	Mean	LLN	Mean	LLN	Mean	LLN	Mean	LLN	Mean	LLN	Mean	LLN	Mean	LLN	Mean	LLN	Mean	LLN	Mean	LLN
145 cm	3.8	2.69	3.61	2.49	3.41	2.29	3.21	2.09	3.01	1.89	2.81	1.69	2.61	1.49	2.41	1.29	2.21	1.09	2.01	0.89	1.81	0.69	1.61	0.49	1.41	0.29
150 cm	3.98	2.78	3.78	2.58	3.58	2.38	3.38	2.18	3.18	1.98	2.98	1.78	2.78	1.58	2.58	1.38	2.38	1.18	2.18	0.98	1.98	0.78	1.78	0.58	1.58	0.38
155 cm	4.15	2.88	3.95	2.68	3.75	2.48	3.55	2.28	3.35	2.08	3.15	1.88	2.95	1.68	2.75	1.48	2.55	1.28	2.35	1.08	2.15	0.88	1.95	0.68	1.75	0.48
160 cm	4.33	2.97	4.13	2.77	3.93	2.57	3.73	2.37	3.53	2.17	3.33	1.97	3.13	1.77	2.93	1.57	2.73	1.37	2.53	1.17	2.33	0.97	2.13	0.77	1.93	0.57
165 cm	4.52	3.07	4.32	2.87	4.12	2.67	3.92	2.47	3.72	2.27	3.52	2.07	3.32	1.87	3.12	1.67	2.92	1.47	2.72	1.27	2.52	1.07	2.32	0.87	2.12	0.67
170 cm	4.71	3.18	4.5	2.98	4.31	2.78	4.11	2.58	3.91	2.38	3.71	2.18	3.51	1.98	3.3	1.78	3.11	1.58	2.91	1.38	2.71	1.18	2.51	0.98	2.31	0.78
175 cm	4.91	3.28	4.71	3.08	4.51	2.88	4.31	2.68	4.11	2.48	3.91	2.28	3.71	2.08	3.51	1.88	3.31	1.68	3.11	1.48	2.91	1.28	2.71	1.08	2.51	0.88
180 cm	5.11	3.39	4.91	3.19	4.71	2.99	4.51	2.79	4.31	2.59	4.11	2.39	3.91	2.19	3.71	1.99	3.51	1.79	3.31	1.59	3.11	1.39	2.91	1.19	2.71	0.99
185 cm	5.32	3.51	5.12	3.3	4.92	3.11	4.72	2.91	4.52	2.71	4.32	2.51	4.12	2.31	3.92	2.11	3.72	1.91	3.52	1.71	3.32	1.51	3.12	1.31	2.92	1.11
190 cm	5.54	3.62	5.34	3.42	5.14	3.22	4.94	3.02	4.74	2.82	4.54	2.62	4.34	2.42	4.14	2.22	3.94	2.02	3.74	1.82	3.54	1.62	3.34	1.42	3.14	1.22
195 cm	5.76	3.74	5.56	3.54	5.36	3.34	5.16	3.14	4.96	2.94	4.76	2.74	4.56	2.54	4.36	2.34	4.16	2.14	3.96	1.94	3.76	1.74	3.56	1.54	3.36	1.34

Table C.1 continued
(Hankinson, Odencrantz & Fedan 1999)

FVC (L) Female

Age (yrs)	18		20		25		30		35		40		45		50		55		60		65		70		75		80	
	Mean	LLN	Mean	LLN	Mean	LLN	Mean	LLN	Mean	LLN	Mean	LLN	Mean	LLN	Mean	LLN	Mean	LLN	Mean	LLN	Mean	LLN	Mean	LLN	Mean	LLN	Mean	LLN
145 cm	2.97	2.42	2.98	2.43	2.99	2.44	2.98	2.43	2.95	2.40	2.90	2.35	2.83	2.28	2.74	2.19	2.63	2.08	2.51	1.96	2.36	1.81	2.20	1.65	2.01	1.46	1.81	1.26
150 cm	3.19	2.60	3.20	2.61	3.21	2.62	3.19	2.61	3.16	2.58	3.11	2.53	3.05	2.46	2.96	2.37	2.85	2.26	2.72	2.14	2.58	1.99	2.41	1.83	2.23	1.64	2.03	1.44
155 cm	3.42	2.79	3.42	2.80	3.43	2.80	3.42	2.79	3.39	2.76	3.34	2.71	3.27	2.64	3.18	2.55	3.08	2.45	2.95	2.32	2.80	2.18	2.64	2.01	2.46	1.83	2.25	1.63
160 cm	3.65	2.98	3.66	2.99	3.67	3.00	3.65	2.98	3.62	2.95	3.57	2.90	3.50	2.83	3.42	2.75	3.31	2.64	3.18	2.51	3.04	2.37	2.87	2.20	2.69	2.02	2.49	1.82
165 cm	3.89	3.18	3.90	3.19	3.91	3.19	3.89	3.18	3.86	3.15	3.81	3.10	3.75	3.03	3.66	2.94	3.55	2.84	3.42	2.71	3.28	2.57	3.11	2.40	2.93	2.22	2.73	2.02
170 cm	4.14	3.38	4.15	3.39	4.15	3.40	4.14	3.39	4.11	3.36	4.06	3.31	3.99	3.24	3.91	3.15	3.80	3.04	3.67	2.92	3.53	2.77	3.36	2.61	3.18	2.42	2.98	2.22
175 cm	4.39	3.59	4.40	3.60	4.41	3.61	4.40	3.60	4.37	3.57	4.32	3.52	4.25	3.45	4.16	3.36	4.05	3.25	3.93	3.13	3.78	2.98	3.62	2.82	3.43	2.63	3.23	2.43
180 cm	4.66	3.81	4.67	3.82	4.67	3.82	4.66	3.81	4.63	3.78	4.58	3.73	4.51	3.66	4.42	3.58	4.32	3.47	4.19	3.34	4.05	3.20	3.88	3.03	3.70	2.85	3.50	2.65
185 cm	4.93	4.03	4.94	4.04	4.94	4.05	4.93	4.04	4.90	4.01	4.85	3.96	4.78	3.89	4.69	3.80	4.59	3.69	4.46	3.57	4.32	3.42	4.15	3.26	3.97	3.07	3.77	2.87
190 cm	5.21	4.26	5.21	4.27	5.22	4.28	5.21	4.26	5.18	4.23	5.13	4.18	5.06	4.12	4.97	4.03	4.87	3.92	4.74	3.79	4.59	3.65	4.43	3.48	4.25	3.30	4.04	3.10
195 cm	5.49	4.50	5.50	4.50	5.51	4.51	5.49	4.50	5.46	4.47	5.41	4.42	5.35	4.35	5.26	4.26	5.15	4.16	5.02	4.03	4.88	3.88	4.71	3.72	4.53	3.54	4.33	3.33

Table C.1 continued
(Hankinson, Odencrantz & Fedan 1999)

FEV₁ (L) Female

Age (yrs)	18		20		25		30		35		40		45		50		55		60		65		70		75		80	
	Mean	LLN	Mean	LLN	Mean	LLN	Mean	LLN	Mean	LLN	Mean	LLN	Mean	LLN	Mean	LLN	Mean	LLN	Mean	LLN	Mean	LLN	Mean	LLN	Mean	LLN	Mean	LLN
145 cm	2.72	2.26	2.70	2.24	2.64	2.17	2.57	2.10	2.49	2.02	2.40	1.93	2.30	1.83	2.18	1.72	2.06	1.60	1.94	1.47	1.80	1.33	1.65	1.18	1.49	1.02	1.32	0.85
150 cm	2.89	2.39	2.87	2.37	2.81	2.31	2.74	2.24	2.66	2.16	2.57	2.07	2.46	1.97	2.35	1.86	2.23	1.74	2.10	1.61	1.97	1.47	1.82	1.32	1.66	1.16	1.49	0.99
155 cm	3.07	2.54	3.05	2.51	2.98	2.45	2.91	2.38	2.83	2.30	2.74	2.21	2.64	2.11	2.53	2.00	2.41	1.88	2.28	1.75	2.14	1.61	1.99	1.46	1.83	1.30	1.66	1.13
160 cm	3.25	2.68	3.23	2.66	3.16	2.60	3.09	2.53	3.01	2.45	2.92	2.35	2.82	2.25	2.71	2.14	2.59	2.02	2.46	1.89	2.32	1.76	2.17	1.61	2.01	1.45	1.85	1.28
165 cm	3.44	2.82	3.41	2.81	3.35	2.75	3.28	2.68	3.20	2.60	3.11	2.51	3.01	2.41	2.90	2.30	2.78	2.18	2.65	2.05	2.51	1.91	2.36	1.76	2.20	1.60	2.03	1.43
170 cm	3.63	2.99	3.61	2.97	3.54	2.90	3.47	2.83	3.39	2.75	3.30	2.66	3.20	2.56	3.09	2.45	2.97	2.33	2.84	2.20	2.70	2.06	2.55	1.91	2.39	1.75	2.23	1.59
175 cm	3.83	3.15	3.80	3.13	3.74	3.06	3.67	2.99	3.59	2.91	3.50	2.82	3.40	2.72	3.29	2.61	3.17	2.49	3.04	2.36	2.90	2.22	2.75	2.07	2.59	1.91	2.42	1.75
180 cm	4.03	3.31	4.01	3.29	3.95	3.23	3.88	3.16	3.79	3.08	3.70	2.99	3.60	2.89	3.49	2.78	3.37	2.66	3.24	2.53	3.10	2.39	2.95	2.24	2.80	2.08	2.63	1.91
185 cm	4.24	3.48	4.22	3.46	4.16	3.40	4.08	3.33	4.00	3.25	3.91	3.16	3.81	3.06	3.70	2.94	3.58	2.83	3.45	2.70	3.31	2.56	3.16	2.41	3.01	2.25	2.84	2.08
190 cm	4.46	3.66	4.43	3.63	4.37	3.57	4.30	3.50	4.22	3.42	4.13	3.33	4.03	3.23	3.92	3.12	3.80	3.00	3.67	2.87	3.53	2.73	3.38	2.58	3.22	2.42	3.05	2.25
195 cm	4.68	3.84	4.65	3.81	4.59	3.75	4.52	3.68	4.44	3.60	4.35	3.51	4.25	3.41	4.14	3.30	4.02	3.18	3.89	3.05	3.75	2.91	3.60	2.76	3.44	2.60	3.27	2.43

Table C.1 continued
(Hankinson, Odencrantz & Fedan 1999)

FEV₁/FVC (%) Female

Age (yrs)	18		20		25		30		35		40		45		50		55		60		65		70		75		80	
	Mean	LLN	Mean	LLN	Mean	LLN	Mean	LLN	Mean	LLN	Mean	LLN	Mean	LLN	Mean	LLN	Mean	LLN	Mean	LLN	Mean	LLN	Mean	LLN	Mean	LLN	Mean	LLN
All heights	87.0	77.2	86.6	76.8	85.5	75.7	84.4	74.6	83.4	73.6	82.3	72.5	81.2	71.5	80.2	70.4	79.1	69.3	78.1	68.3	77.0	67.2	75.9	66.1	74.9	65.1	73.8	64.0

Table C.1 continued
(Hankinson, Odencrantz & Fedan 1999)

FEF$_{25-75\%}$ (L/sec) Female

Age (yrs)	18		20		25		30		35		40		45		50		55		60		65		70		75		80	
	Mean	LLN	Mean	LLN	Mean	LLN	Mean	LLN	Mean	LLN	Mean	LLN	Mean	LLN	Mean	LLN	Mean	LLN	Mean	LLN	Mean	LLN	Mean	LLN	Mean	LLN	Mean	LLN
145 cm	3.43	2.44	3.37	2.39	3.23	2.25	3.08	2.10	2.92	1.94	2.75	1.77	2.57	1.59	2.38	1.40	2.18	1.20	1.97	0.99	1.75	0.77	1.52	0.54	1.28	0.30	1.03	0.05
150 cm	3.53	2.48	3.48	2.42	3.34	2.28	3.19	2.13	3.03	1.97	2.86	1.80	2.68	1.62	2.49	1.43	2.29	1.23	2.08	1.02	1.86	0.80	1.63	0.57	1.38	0.33	1.13	0.08
155 cm	3.64	2.51	3.58	2.46	3.44	2.32	3.29	2.17	3.13	2.01	2.96	1.84	2.78	1.66	2.59	1.47	2.39	1.27	2.18	1.06	1.96	0.84	1.73	0.61	1.49	0.37	1.24	0.12
160 cm	3.75	2.55	3.69	2.50	3.55	2.36	3.40	2.21	3.24	2.04	3.07	1.87	2.89	1.69	2.70	1.50	2.50	1.30	2.29	1.09	2.07	0.87	1.84	0.64	1.60	0.40	1.35	0.15
165 cm	3.86	2.59	3.81	2.53	3.67	2.39	3.52	2.24	3.36	2.08	3.19	1.91	3.01	1.73	2.82	1.54	2.62	1.34	2.41	1.13	2.19	0.91	1.96	0.68	1.71	0.44	1.46	0.19
170 cm	3.98	2.62	3.92	2.57	3.78	2.43	3.63	2.28	3.47	2.12	3.30	1.95	3.12	1.77	2.93	1.58	2.73	1.38	2.52	1.17	2.30	0.95	2.07	0.72	1.83	0.48	1.58	0.23
175 cm	4.10	2.66	4.04	2.61	3.90	2.47	3.75	2.32	3.59	2.16	3.42	1.99	3.24	1.81	3.05	1.62	2.85	1.42	2.64	1.21	2.42	0.99	2.19	0.76	1.95	0.52	1.70	0.27
180 cm	4.22	2.71	4.17	2.65	4.03	2.51	3.88	2.36	3.72	2.20	3.55	2.03	3.37	1.85	3.18	1.66	2.98	1.46	2.77	1.25	2.55	1.03	2.32	0.80	2.08	0.56	1.83	0.31
185 cm	4.35	2.75	4.30	2.69	4.16	2.55	4.01	2.40	3.85	2.24	3.67	2.07	3.49	1.89	3.30	1.70	3.10	1.50	2.89	1.29	2.67	1.07	2.44	0.84	2.20	0.60	1.95	0.35
190 cm	4.48	2.79	4.43	2.74	4.29	2.60	4.14	2.45	3.98	2.29	3.81	2.12	3.63	1.94	3.44	1.75	3.24	1.55	3.03	1.34	2.80	1.12	2.57	0.89	2.33	0.65	2.08	0.39
195 cm	4.61	2.83	4.56	2.78	4.42	2.64	4.27	2.49	4.11	2.33	3.94	2.16	3.76	1.98	3.57	1.79	3.37	1.59	3.16	1.38	2.94	1.16	2.71	0.93	2.47	0.69	2.22	0.44

Table C.1 continued
(Hankinson, Odencrantz & Fedan 1999)

PEF (L/min) Female

Age (yrs)	18		20		25		30		35		40		45		50		55		60		65		70		75		80	
	Mean	LLN	Mean	LLN	Mean	LLN	Mean	LLN	Mean	LLN	Mean	LLN	Mean	LLN	Mean	LLN	Mean	LLN	Mean	LLN	Mean	LLN	Mean	LLN	Mean	LLN	Mean	LLN
145 cm	345	264	349	267	356	274	360	278	360	279	358	276	352	271	344	262	332	250	317	236	299	218	278	197	254	173	227	146
150 cm	362	274	365	278	372	285	376	289	377	289	374	287	369	281	360	273	349	261	334	246	316	228	295	208	271	183	244	156
155 cm	379	286	382	289	389	296	393	300	394	300	391	298	386	293	377	284	366	272	351	257	333	240	312	219	288	195	261	167
160 cm	396	297	400	301	407	307	411	311	411	312	409	310	403	304	395	295	383	284	368	269	351	251	330	230	305	206	278	179
165 cm	415	309	418	312	425	319	429	323	430	324	427	321	422	316	413	307	401	296	387	281	369	263	348	242	324	218	296	191
170 cm	433	321	437	325	444	332	448	335	448	336	446	334	440	328	432	319	420	308	405	293	387	275	366	254	342	230	315	203
175 cm	453	334	456	337	463	344	467	348	468	349	465	346	460	341	451	332	439	320	425	306	407	288	386	267	362	243	334	216
180 cm	472	347	476	350	483	357	487	361	487	361	485	359	479	354	471	345	459	333	444	319	427	301	406	280	381	256	354	228
185 cm	493	360	496	363	503	370	507	374	508	375	505	372	500	367	491	358	480	347	465	332	447	314	426	293	402	269	375	242
190 cm	514	374	517	377	524	384	528	388	529	388	526	386	521	381	512	372	501	360	486	345	468	328	447	307	423	283	396	255
195 cm	535	388	539	391	546	398	550	402	550	402	548	400	542	395	534	386	522	374	507	360	489	342	468	321	444	297	417	269

Table C.1 continued
(Hankinson, Crapo & Jensen 2003)

FVC$_6$ (L) Female

Age (yrs)	18 Mean	18 LLN	20 Mean	20 LLN	25 Mean	25 LLN	30 Mean	30 LLN	35 Mean	35 LLN	40 Mean	40 LLN	45 Mean	45 LLN	50 Mean	50 LLN	55 Mean	55 LLN	60 Mean	60 LLN	65 Mean	65 LLN	70 Mean	70 LLN	75 Mean	75 LLN	80 Mean	80 LLN
145 cm	3.00	2.48	3.00	2.47	2.98	2.46	2.95	2.42	2.89	2.37	2.82	2.30	2.74	2.21	2.63	2.11	2.51	1.99	2.37	1.85	2.22	1.70	2.05	1.52	1.86	1.33	1.65	1.13
150 cm	3.22	2.66	3.21	2.65	3.20	2.64	3.16	2.60	3.11	2.55	3.04	2.48	2.95	2.39	2.85	2.29	2.73	2.17	2.59	2.03	2.44	1.88	2.26	1.70	2.07	1.51	1.86	1.30
155 cm	3.44	2.84	3.44	2.84	3.42	2.82	3.39	2.79	3.33	2.74	3.26	2.67	3.18	2.58	3.07	2.48	2.95	2.35	2.81	2.22	2.66	2.06	2.49	1.89	2.30	1.70	2.09	1.49
160 cm	3.67	3.03	3.67	3.03	3.65	3.01	3.62	2.98	3.56	2.92	3.49	2.86	3.41	2.77	3.30	2.67	3.18	2.55	3.04	2.41	2.89	2.25	2.72	2.08	2.53	1.89	2.32	1.68
165 cm	3.91	3.23	3.91	3.23	3.89	3.21	3.85	3.18	3.80	3.12	3.73	3.05	3.65	2.97	3.54	2.86	3.42	2.74	3.28	2.61	3.13	2.45	2.95	2.28	2.76	2.09	2.56	1.88
170 cm	4.15	3.43	4.15	3.43	4.13	3.41	4.10	3.38	4.05	3.33	3.98	3.26	3.89	3.17	3.79	3.07	3.67	2.95	3.53	2.81	3.37	2.65	3.20	2.48	3.01	2.29	2.80	2.08
175 cm	4.41	3.64	4.40	3.64	4.39	3.62	4.35	3.59	4.30	3.54	4.23	3.47	4.14	3.38	4.04	3.28	3.92	3.16	3.73	3.02	3.63	2.86	3.45	2.69	3.26	2.50	3.06	2.29
180 cm	4.67	3.86	4.66	3.85	4.65	3.84	4.61	3.81	4.56	3.75	4.49	3.68	4.40	3.60	4.30	3.49	4.18	3.37	4.04	3.23	3.89	3.08	3.71	2.91	3.52	2.72	3.32	2.51
185 cm	4.93	4.08	4.93	4.08	4.91	4.06	4.88	4.03	4.83	3.98	4.76	3.91	4.67	3.82	4.57	3.72	4.45	3.59	4.31	3.46	4.15	3.30	3.98	3.13	3.79	2.94	3.58	2.73
190 cm	5.21	4.31	5.21	4.31	5.19	4.29	5.15	4.26	5.10	4.20	5.03	4.13	4.95	4.05	4.84	3.94	4.72	3.82	4.58	3.68	4.43	3.53	4.25	3.36	4.06	3.17	3.86	2.96
195 cm	5.49	4.54	5.49	4.54	5.47	4.52	5.44	4.49	5.38	4.44	5.31	4.37	5.23	4.28	5.12	4.18	5.00	4.06	4.87	3.92	4.71	3.76	4.54	3.59	4.35	3.40	4.14	3.19

Table C.1 continued
(Hankinson, Crapo & Jensen 2003)

FEV₁/FVC₆ (%) Female

Age (yrs)	18		20		25		30		35		40		45		50		55		60		65		70		75		80	
	Mean	LLN	Mean	LLN	Mean	LLN	Mean	LLN	Mean	LLN	Mean	LLN	Mean	LLN	Mean	LLN	Mean	LLN	Mean	LLN	Mean	LLN	Mean	LLN	Mean	LLN	Mean	LLN
All heights	87.2	78.5	86.9	78.2	86.1	77.4	85.3	76.7	84.6	75.9	83.8	75.1	83.0	74.3	82.2	73.5	81.4	72.7	80.6	71.9	79.8	71.1	79.0	70.3	78.2	69.5	77.4	68.8

Table C.1 continued
(Hankinson, Crapo & Jensen 2003)

FEF$_{25-75\%}$ (L/sec) Female

Age (yrs)	18		20		25		30		35		40		45		50		55		60		65		70		75		80	
	Mean	LLN	Mean	LLN	Mean	LLN	Mean	LLN	Mean	LLN	Mean	LLN	Mean	LLN	Mean	LLN	Mean	LLN	Mean	LLN	Mean	LLN	Mean	LLN	Mean	LLN	Mean	LLN
145 cm	3.52	2.50	3.45	2.44	3.28	2.27	3.11	2.10	2.94	1.93	2.77	1.76	2.60	1.59	2.43	1.42	2.26	1.25	2.09	1.08	1.92	0.91	1.75	0.74	1.58	0.57	1.41	0.40
150 cm	3.65	2.56	3.58	2.49	3.41	2.32	3.24	2.15	3.07	1.98	2.90	1.81	2.73	1.64	2.56	1.47	2.39	1.30	2.22	1.13	2.05	0.96	1.88	0.79	1.71	0.62	1.54	0.45
155 cm	3.78	2.62	3.71	2.55	3.54	2.38	3.37	2.21	3.20	2.04	3.03	1.87	2.86	1.70	2.69	1.53	2.52	1.36	2.35	1.19	2.18	1.02	2.01	0.85	1.84	0.68	1.67	0.51
160 cm	3.92	2.58	3.85	2.61	3.68	2.44	3.51	2.27	3.34	2.10	3.17	1.93	3.00	1.76	2.83	1.59	2.66	1.42	2.49	1.25	2.32	1.08	2.15	0.91	1.98	0.74	1.81	0.57
165 cm	4.06	2.75	3.99	2.68	3.82	2.51	3.65	2.34	3.48	2.17	3.31	2.00	3.14	1.83	2.97	1.66	2.80	1.49	2.63	1.32	2.46	1.15	2.29	0.98	2.12	0.81	1.95	0.64
170 cm	4.21	2.81	4.14	2.74	3.97	2.57	3.80	2.40	3.63	2.23	3.46	2.06	3.29	1.89	3.12	1.72	2.95	1.55	2.78	1.38	2.61	1.21	2.44	1.04	2.27	0.87	2.10	0.70
175 cm	4.36	2.88	4.29	2.81	4.12	2.64	3.95	2.47	3.78	2.30	3.61	2.13	3.44	1.96	3.27	1.79	3.10	1.62	2.93	1.45	2.76	1.28	2.59	1.11	2.42	0.94	2.25	0.77
180 cm	4.51	2.95	4.44	2.88	4.27	2.71	4.10	2.54	3.93	2.37	3.76	2.20	3.59	2.03	3.42	1.86	3.25	1.69	3.08	1.52	2.91	1.35	2.74	1.18	2.57	1.01	2.40	0.84
185 cm	4.67	3.02	4.60	2.95	4.43	2.78	4.26	2.61	4.09	2.44	3.92	2.27	3.75	2.10	3.58	1.93	3.41	1.76	3.24	1.59	3.07	1.42	2.90	1.25	2.73	1.08	2.56	0.91
190 cm	4.84	3.09	4.77	3.03	4.60	2.86	4.43	2.69	4.26	2.52	4.09	2.35	3.92	2.18	3.75	2.01	3.58	1.84	3.41	1.67	3.24	1.50	3.07	1.33	2.90	1.16	2.73	0.99
195 cm	5.00	3.12	4.94	3.10	4.77	2.93	4.60	2.76	4.43	2.59	4.26	2.42	4.09	2.25	3.92	2.08	3.75	1.91	3.58	1.74	3.41	1.57	3.24	1.40	3.07	1.23	2.90	1.06

Table C.1 continued
(Hankinson, Odencrantz & Fedan 1999)

FEV$_1$ (L) Male children

Age (yrs)	8		10		12		14		16		18		20	
	Mean	LLN	Mean	LLN	Mean	LLN	Mean	LLN	Mean	LLN	Mean	LLN	Mean	LLN
120 cm	1.24	0.88	1.32	0.96	1.44	1.08	1.59	1.23	1.77	1.42	2.00	1.64	2.25	1.90
125 cm	1.42	1.03	1.49	1.11	1.61	1.22	1.76	1.37	1.95	1.56	2.17	1.78	2.43	2.04
130 cm	1.60	1.17	1.67	1.25	1.79	1.37	1.94	1.52	2.13	1.71	2.35	1.93	2.61	2.19
135 cm	1.78	1.33	1.86	1.41	1.98	1.52	2.13	1.67	2.31	1.86	2.54	2.08	2.79	2.34
140 cm	1.98	1.49	2.06	1.57	2.17	1.68	2.32	1.83	2.51	2.02	2.73	2.24	2.99	2.50
145 cm	2.18	1.65	2.26	1.73	2.37	1.85	2.52	2.00	2.71	2.18	2.93	2.41	3.19	2.66
150 cm	2.38	1.82	2.46	1.90	2.58	2.02	2.73	2.17	2.92	2.36	3.14	2.58	3.40	2.84
155 cm	2.60	2.00	2.68	2.08	2.79	2.20	2.94	2.35	3.13	2.53	3.35	2.75	3.61	3.01
160 cm	2.82	2.18	2.90	2.26	3.02	2.38	3.17	2.53	3.35	2.72	3.58	2.94	3.83	3.20
165 cm	3.05	2.37	3.13	2.45	3.24	2.57	3.40	2.72	3.58	2.90	3.80	3.13	4.06	3.38
170 cm	3.29	2.57	3.37	2.65	3.48	2.76	3.63	2.91	3.82	3.10	4.04	3.32	4.30	3.58
175 cm	3.53	2.77	3.61	2.85	3.72	2.96	3.87	3.11	4.06	3.30	4.28	3.52	4.54	3.78
180 cm	3.78	2.97	3.86	3.05	3.97	3.17	4.13	3.32	4.31	3.50	4.53	3.73	4.79	3.98
185 cm	4.04	3.19	4.12	3.26	4.23	3.38	4.38	3.53	4.57	3.72	4.79	3.94	5.05	4.20

FVC (L) Male children

Age (yrs)	8		10		12		14		16		18		20	
	Mean	LLN	Mean	LLN	Mean	LLN	Mean	LLN	Mean	LLN	Mean	LLN	Mean	LLN
130 cm	1.91	1.41	1.86	1.37	1.90	1.40	2.02	1.52	2.22	1.72	2.50	2.00	2.86	2.36
135 cm	2.15	1.62	2.11	1.57	2.15	1.61	2.27	1.73	2.47	1.93	2.75	2.21	3.11	2.57
140 cm	2.41	1.83	2.37	1.79	2.40	1.83	2.52	1.95	2.72	2.15	3.00	2.43	3.37	2.79
145 cm	2.68	2.06	2.63	2.01	2.67	2.05	2.79	2.17	2.99	2.37	3.27	2.65	3.63	3.01
150 cm	2.95	2.29	2.91	2.24	2.95	2.28	3.06	2.40	3.26	2.60	3.54	2.88	3.91	3.24
155 cm	3.24	2.53	3.19	2.48	3.23	2.52	3.35	2.64	3.55	2.84	3.83	3.12	4.19	3.48
160 cm	3.53	2.77	3.49	2.73	3.52	2.77	3.64	2.89	3.84	3.09	4.12	3.37	4.48	3.73
165 cm	3.83	3.03	3.79	2.99	3.83	3.02	3.94	3.14	4.14	3.34	4.43	3.62	4.79	3.98
170 cm	4.14	3.29	4.10	3.25	4.14	3.29	4.26	3.41	4.46	3.61	4.74	3.89	5.10	4.25
175 cm	4.47	3.56	4.42	3.52	4.46	3.56	4.58	3.68	4.78	3.88	5.06	4.16	5.42	4.52
180 cm	4.80	3.84	4.75	3.80	4.79	3.84	4.91	3.95	5.11	4.15	5.39	4.44	5.75	4.80
185 cm	5.14	4.13	5.09	4.09	5.13	4.12	5.25	4.24	5.45	4.44	5.73	4.72	6.09	5.08

Table C.1 continued
(Hankinson, Odencrantz & Fedan 1999)

FEV_1/FVC (%) Male children

Age (yrs)	8		10		12		14		16		18		20	
	Mean	LLN	Mean	LLN	Mean	LLN	Mean	LLN	Mean	LLN	Mean	LLN	Mean	LLN
All heights	86.4	76.7	86.0	76.3	85.6	75.9	85.2	75.5	84.8	75.1	84.3	74.7	83.9	74.3

PEF (L/min) Male children

Age (yrs)	8		10		12		14		16		18		20	
	Mean	LLN	Mean	LLN	Mean	LLN	Mean	LLN	Mean	LLN	Mean	LLN	Mean	LLN
130 cm	208	134	222	148	242	168	268	194	300	226	339	265	384	310
135 cm	228	148	242	162	262	182	288	208	320	240	359	279	404	324
140 cm	249	163	262	176	282	196	308	222	341	255	380	294	425	339
145 cm	270	178	284	191	304	211	330	237	362	270	401	309	446	354
150 cm	292	193	306	207	326	227	352	253	384	285	423	324	468	369
155 cm	315	210	329	223	349	243	375	269	407	302	446	340	491	385
160 cm	339	226	352	240	372	260	398	286	431	318	470	357	515	402
165 cm	363	243	377	257	396	277	423	303	455	335	494	374	539	419
170 cm	388	261	402	275	422	295	448	321	480	353	519	392	564	437
175 cm	414	279	428	293	447	313	474	339	506	371	545	410	590	455
180 cm	441	298	454	312	474	332	500	358	533	390	571	429	616	474
185 cm	468	317	481	331	501	351	527	377	560	409	599	448	644	493

FEV$_1$ (L) Female children

Age (yrs)	8		10		12		14		16		18	
	Mean	LLN	Mean	LLN	Mean	LLN	Mean	LLN	Mean	LLN	Mean	LLN
120 cm	1.31	0.99	1.44	1.12	1.57	1.25	1.70	1.38	1.83	1.51	1.96	1.64
125 cm	1.45	1.10	1.58	1.23	1.71	1.36	1.84	1.49	1.97	1.63	2.10	1.76
130 cm	1.59	1.22	1.73	1.35	1.86	1.48	1.99	1.61	2.12	1.74	2.25	1.87
135 cm	1.75	1.34	1.88	1.47	2.01	1.61	2.14	1.74	2.27	1.87	2.40	2.00
140 cm	1.91	1.47	2.04	1.60	2.17	1.73	2.30	1.86	2.43	1.99	2.56	2.13
145 cm	2.07	1.60	2.20	1.73	2.33	1.87	2.46	2.00	2.59	2.13	2.72	2.26
150 cm	2.24	1.74	2.37	1.87	2.50	2.00	2.63	2.13	2.76	2.26	2.89	2.39
155 cm	2.41	1.88	2.54	2.01	2.68	2.14	2.81	2.27	2.94	2.41	3.07	2.54
160 cm	2.59	2.03	2.73	2.16	2.86	2.29	2.99	2.42	3.12	2.55	3.25	2.68
165 cm	2.78	2.18	2.91	2.31	3.04	2.44	3.17	2.57	3.30	2.70	3.44	2.83
170 cm	2.97	2.33	3.11	2.47	3.24	2.60	3.37	2.73	3.50	2.86	3.63	2.99
175 cm	3.17	2.49	3.30	2.63	3.43	2.76	3.56	2.89	3.70	3.02	3.83	3.15
180 cm	3.38	2.66	3.51	2.79	3.64	2.92	3.77	3.05	3.90	3.18	4.03	3.31
185 cm	3.59	2.83	3.72	2.96	3.85	3.09	3.98	3.22	4.11	3.35	4.24	3.48

FVC (L) Female children

Age (yrs)	8		10		12		14		16		18	
	Mean	LLN	Mean	LLN	Mean	LLN	Mean	LLN	Mean	LLN	Mean	LLN
120 cm	1.40	1.02	1.52	1.14	1.64	1.26	1.75	1.38	1.87	1.49	1.99	1.61
125 cm	1.58	1.17	1.70	1.29	1.82	1.41	1.93	1.53	2.05	1.64	2.17	1.76
130 cm	1.77	1.33	1.89	1.44	2.01	1.56	2.12	1.68	2.24	1.80	2.36	1.92
135 cm	1.97	1.49	2.08	1.61	2.20	1.72	2.32	1.84	2.44	1.96	2.56	2.08
140 cm	2.17	1.66	2.29	1.77	2.41	1.89	2.52	2.01	2.64	2.13	2.76	2.25
145 cm	2.38	1.83	2.50	1.95	2.62	2.07	2.73	2.18	2.85	2.30	2.97	2.42
150 cm	2.60	2.01	2.72	2.13	2.84	2.25	2.95	2.36	3.07	2.48	3.19	2.60
155 cm	2.82	2.20	2.94	2.31	3.06	2.43	3.18	2.55	3.30	2.67	3.42	2.79
160 cm	3.06	2.39	3.18	2.51	3.29	2.62	3.41	2.74	3.53	2.86	3.65	2.98
165 cm	3.30	2.59	3.42	2.70	3.54	2.82	3.65	2.94	3.77	3.06	3.89	3.18
170 cm	3.55	2.79	3.66	2.91	3.78	3.03	3.90	3.15	4.02	3.26	4.14	3.38
175 cm	3.80	3.00	3.92	3.12	4.04	3.24	4.16	3.36	4.28	3.47	4.39	3.59
180 cm	4.07	3.22	4.18	3.34	4.30	3.45	4.42	3.57	4.54	3.69	4.66	3.81
185 cm	4.34	3.44	4.45	3.56	4.57	3.68	4.69	3.79	4.81	3.91	4.93	4.03

Table C.1 continued
(Hankinson, Odencrantz & Fedan 1999)

FEV$_1$/FVC (%) Female children

Age (yrs)	8		10		12		14		16		18	
	Mean	LLN	Mean	LLN	Mean	LLN	Mean	LLN	Mean	LLN	Mean	LLN
All heights	89.1	79.3	88.7	78.9	88.3	78.5	87.8	78.0	87.4	77.6	87.0	77.2

PEF (L/min) Female children

Age (yrs)	8		10		12		14		16		18	
	Mean	LLN	Mean	LLN	Mean	LLN	Mean	LLN	Mean	LLN	Mean	LLN
120 cm	170	114	207	151	235	179	255	199	267	211	271	215
125 cm	184	123	220	160	249	188	269	208	281	220	285	224
130 cm	198	132	235	169	263	197	283	217	295	230	299	234
135 cm	213	142	249	179	278	207	298	227	310	239	314	243
140 cm	228	152	265	189	293	217	313	237	325	249	329	253
145 cm	244	163	281	199	309	227	329	247	341	260	345	264
150 cm	261	173	297	210	325	238	346	258	358	270	362	274
155 cm	278	184	314	221	342	249	363	269	375	281	379	285
160 cm	295	196	332	232	360	261	380	281	392	293	396	297
165 cm	314	208	350	244	378	272	398	293	411	305	415	309
170 cm	332	220	369	256	397	285	417	305	429	317	433	321
175 cm	352	233	388	269	416	297	436	317	449	330	453	334
180 cm	371	245	408	282	436	310	456	330	468	342	472	347
185 cm	392	259	428	295	456	323	477	344	489	356	493	360

Glossary

ANZSRS   Australian and New Zealand Society of Respiratory Science. (www.anzsrs.org.au)

ATPS   Atmospheric temperature and pressure saturated with water vapour.

ATS   American Thoracic Society. (www.thoracic.org)

Back-extrapolation   Procedure applied to the maximal expiratory spirogram (volume versus time) to determine zero time. The zero time point is the point on the time axis where exhalation would have started, assuming 'instantaneous' flow acceleration (the patient's maximal flow is projected back to the volume axis) and is used for the calculation of FEV_1.

BTPS   Body temperature (37°C) and pressure saturated with water vapour (47 mmHg). All volumes and flows are reported after conversion to BTPS conditions.

ERS   European Respiratory Society. (www.ersnet.org)

$FEF_{25-75\%}$ Forced expiratory flow over the middle half of the FVC manoeuvre. This is the average expired flow over

the middle half of the FVC manoeuv
Normally reported in L/s. In Europ
this is often referred to as the
$MEF_{25-75\%}$ or MMEF (maximum mid-
expiratory flow).

$FEF_{25-75\%6}$ Forced expiratory flow over the middle
half of the FVC_6 manoevre. Normally
reported in L/s.

$FEF_{50\%}$ Forced expiratory flow at 50% of the
FVC. This is the maximal expiratory
flow measured at the point where 50%
of the FVC has been expired. Normally
reported in L/s. In Europe this is often
referred to as the $MEF_{50\%}$.

$FEF_{75\%}$ Forced expiratory flow at 75% FVC.
This is the maximal expiratory flow
measured at the point where 75% has
been expired. Normally reported in
L/s. In Europe this is often referred to
as the $MEF_{25\%}$.

FET   Forced expiratory time. This is the time
(in seconds) required to perform the
FVC manoeuvre.

FEV_1 Forced expired volume in 1 second. This
is the volume expired (in L or mL) in the
first second of maximal expiration
(initiated after a maximal inspiration).

FEV_1/FVC ratio   The FEV_1 expressed as a percentage of
(FEV_1/VC)   the VC or FVC. The normal ratio is
about 75 to 85%. Lung disease can
increase or decrease the ratio. This is
also referred to as the forced expiratory
ratio, FER%.

FEV_6 Similar to FVC_6 but is the forced
expired volume measured *at* 6 seconds.

FEV_1/FVC_6 ratio FEV_1 expressed as a percentage of the
FVC_6. Lung disease can increase or
decrease this ratio.

FIV_1 Forced inspired volume in 1 second (L
or mL). Maximum volume that can be

	inspired from residual volume in 1 second.
FIVC	Forced inspired vital capacity (L or mL). Maximum volume that can be inspired from residual volume.
Flow-volume loop	A plot of maximal expired and inspired volume versus flow. Most of the expiratory curve is effort-independent and the entire inspiratory curve is effort-dependent.
FRC	Function residual capacity (L or mL), that is, the resting volume of the lungs.
FVC	Forced vital capacity (L or mL). The maximum volume of air that can be expired or inspired during a forced expiratory manoeuvre initiated from TLC or RV.
FVC_6	Largest forced expiratory volume (L or mL) measured during the first 6 seconds.
Hyperinflation	This term refers to a significant increase in static lung volumes—total lung capacity, or functional residual capacity, or residual volume. Dynamic increase in functional residual capacity can occur particularly in subjects with airflow obstruction when expiratory time is insufficient, for instance when breathing rate is increased during exercise.
Inspiratory capacity (IC)	The maximum volume of air that can be inspired from functional residual capacity. Normally reported in L or mL.
Kymograph	Rotating drum used with manual displacement spirometers to record time and respired volume.
Methacholine chloride	Non-specific bronchial agent that can induce airway constriction. The dose of methacholine that induces a 20% decrease in FEV_1 from the control value is referred to as the $PD_{20\%}$.

Mixed ventilatory defect	Characterised by *both* airflow limitation (obstruction) and loss of lung volume (lung restriction). Produces both a low FEV_1/FVC ratio and low VC (or FVC). The restrictive component should be confirmed and quantified by formal measurement of lung volume (for example multi-breath inert gas dilution, nitrogen washout or whole body plethysmography).
NAC	National Asthma Council of Australia. (www.nationalasthma.org.au).
Obstructive ventilatory defect	Characterised by airflow limitation, for example reduced FEV_1, FEV_1/FVC ratio or PEF. The term 'airflow limitation' is also used and is, perhaps, a more accurate term than 'obstruction' as reduced expired flows can arise not only due to abnormal airway calibre, but also in altered parenchymal compliance and impaired mechanical linkage between airways and lung parenchyma.
P_b	Barometric pressure (mmHg).
$PD_{20\%}$	Dose of provoking agent (for example, methacholine) required to decrease the FEV_1 (or PEF) by 20% from the baseline value.
PEF	Peak expiratory flow (L/s or L/min). This is the maximal expiratory flow achieved during a maximum forced expiration initiated at TLC. The PEF occurs very early in the forced expiratory manoeuvre.
PIF	Peak inspiratory flow (L/s or L/min). This is the maximal inspiratory flow achieved during a maximum forced inspiration initiated at residual volume.
Pneumotachometer or pneumotachograph	Device for measuring flow from the pressure drop across a uniform and

	known resistance under conditions of laminar flow.
Restrictive ventilatory defect	Characterised by loss of lung volume in the absence of airflow limitation, as suggested by a low VC or FVC but normal or high FEV_1/FVC ratio. If lung restriction is suspected on spirometry, formal measurements of lung volumes should be done to confirm and quantify it (for example multi-breath inert gas dilution, nitrogen washout or whole body plethysmography).
Reversibility	Improvement in ventilatory function (for instance, FEV_1) following the inhalation of a bronchodilator:

$$\% \text{ improvement} = 100 \times \frac{FEV_1 \text{ (post–bronchodilator)} - FEV_1 \text{ (baseline)}}{FEV_1 \text{ (baseline)}}$$

Significant reversibility is implied if there is a $\geq 12\%$ improvement in FEV_1 (or FVC) *and* an absolute improvement of ≥ 0.2 L.

Spirogram	A plot of respired volume versus time.
Spirometer	Device used to measure respired volume. Spirometers may be classified as either volume or flow spirometers depending on whether the primary signal measured is volume or flow.
Spirometry	Physiological test to measure the ventilatory function of the lungs.
TLC	Total lung capacity (L or mL). Total volume contained within the lung at full inspiration.
TSANZ	Thoracic Society of Australia and New Zealand. (www.thoracic.org.au)
VC	Vital capacity (L or mL). The maximum volume of air that can be expired or inspired during a slow manoeuvre initiated at TLC or residual volume, respectively.

References

References

American Thoracic Society, 'Standardization of spirometry, 1994 update', *American Journal of Respiratory and Critical Care Medicine*, 1995, vol. 152, pp. 1107–36.

Burton D, Johns DP and Swanney M, *Spirometer Users' and Buyers' Guide*, 2005, Australian Government Department of Health and Ageing, published online at www.nationalasthma.org.au

Crapo RO, 'Pulmonary function testing', *New England Journal of Medicine*, 1994, vol. 331, pp. 25–30.

Enright PL, Connett JE and Bailey WC, 'The FEV_1/FEV_6 predicts lung function decline in adult smokers', *Respiratory Medicine*, 2002, vol. 96, pp. 444–9.

Fardy HJ, 'Asthma update: spirometry; value adding in GP asthma care', *GP Review*, September 2001, p. 21.

Ferguson GT, Enright PL, Buist AS and Higgins MW, 'Office spirometry for health assessment in adults: a consensus statement from the National Lung Health Education Program, *Chest*, 2000, vol. 117, pp. 1146–61.

Hankinson JL, Odencrantz JR and Fedan KB, 'Spirometric reference values from a sample of the general US population', *American Journal of Respiratory and Critical Care Medicine*, 1999, vol. 159, pp. 179–87.

Hankinson JL, Crapo RO and Jensen RL, 'Spirometric reference values for the 6-s FVC maneuver', *Chest*, 2003, vol. 124, pp. 1805–11.

Johns DP, Ingram C, Booth H, Williams TJ and Walters EH, 'Effect of a micro-aerosol filter on the measurement of lung function', *Chest*, 1995, vol. 107, pp. 1045–8.

DP, Hartley MF, Burns G and Thompson BR, 'Variation in barometric pressure in Melbourne does not significantly affect the BTPS correction factor', *Respirology*, 2004, vol. 9, pp. 406–8.

Kendrick AH, Johns DP and Leeming JP, 'Infection control of lung function equipment: a practical approach', *Respiratory Medicine*, 2003, vol. 97, no. 11, pp. 1163–79.

Miller MR, Crapo R, Hankinson J, Brusasco V, Burgos F, Casaburi R, Coates A, Enright P, van der Grinten CPM, Gustafsson P, Jensen R, Johnson DC, MacIntyre N, McKay R, Navajas D, Pedersen OF, Pellegrino R, Viegi G and Wanger J, 'General considerations for lung function testing', *European Respiratory Journal*, 2005a, vol. 26, pp. 153–62.

Miller MR, Hankinson J, Brusasco V, Burgos F, Casaburi R, Coates A, Crapo RO, Enright P, van der Grinten CPM, Gustafsson P, Jensen R, Johnson DC, MacIntyre N, McKay R, Navajas D, Pedersen OF, Pellegrino R, Viegi G and Wanger J, 'Standardisation of spirometry', *European Respiratory Journal*, 2005b, vol. 26, pp. 319–38.

National Asthma Council Australia, *Asthma Management Handbook*, 2006, Melbourne, Australia.

O'Donnell DE, 'Assessment of Bronchodilator Efficacy in Symptomatic COPD', *Chest*, 2000, 117, pp. 42–7S.

Pellegrino R, Viegi G, Brusasco V, Crapo RO, Burgos F, Casaburi R, Coates A, van der Grinten CPM, Gustafsson P, Hankinson J, Jensen R, Johnson DC, MacIntyre N, McKay R, Miller MR, Navajas D, Pedersen OF and Wanger J, 'Interpretative strategies for lung function tests', *European Respiratory Journal*, 2005, 26, pp. 948–68.

Pierce R and Johns DP, Spirometry: *The Measurement and Interpretation of Ventilatory Function in Clinical Practice*, 1995, National Asthma Campaign, available online at www.nationalasthma.org.au

Quanjer PhH, Tammeling GJ, Cotes JE, Pedersen OF, Peslin R and Yernault JC, *Lung Volumes and Forced Ventilatory Flows*, Report working party: Standardization of lung function tests, European Community for Steel and Coal, European Respiratory Society, 1993, 6, Suppl., 16, pp. 4–40.

Side EA, Harrington G, Thien F, Walters EH and Johns DP, 'A cost-analysis of two approaches to infection control in a lung function laboratory', *Australian and New Zealand Journal of Medicine*, 1999, 29, pp. 9–14.

Swanney MP, Jensen RL, Crichton DA, Beckert LE, Cardno LA and Crapo RO, 'FEV$_6$ is an acceptable surrogate for FVC in the spirometric diagnosis of airway obstruction and restriction', *American Journal of Respiratory Critical Care Medicine*, 2000, 162, pp. 917–19.

Unstead M, Stearn MD, Cramer D, Chadwick MV and Wilson R, 'An audit into the efficacy of single use bacterial/viral filters for the prevention of equipment contamination during lung function assessment', *Respiratory Medicine*, 2006, 100, pp. 946–50.

Useful websites

- American Association for Respiratory Care: www.aarc.org
- American College of Chest Physicians (ACCP): www.chestnet.org
- American Lung Association: www.lungusa.org
- American Thoracic Society: www.thoracic.org
- Asian Pacific Society of Respirology: www.apsresp.org
- Association for Respiratory Technology & Physiology: www.artp.org.uk
- Australian & New Zealand Society of Respiratory Science Inc.: www.anzsrs.org.au
- Australian Lung Foundation: www.lungnet.org.au
- British Thoracic Society: www.brit-thoracic.org.uk
- Canadian Thoracic Society: www.lung.ca/cts
- European Respiratory Society: www.ersnet.org
- National Asthma Council Australia: www.nationalasthma.org.au
- National Health and Medical Research Council: www.nhmrc.gov.au
- National Heart, Lung and Blood Institute (NHLBI): www.nhlbi.nih.gov/index.htm
- *Spirometer Users' and Buyers' Guide*: www.nationalasthma.org.au/HTML/management/spiro_guide/index.asp
- The Canadian Society of Respiratory Therapists: www.csrt.com
- The Thoracic Society of Australia & New Zealand: www.thoracic.org.au
- World Health Organization (WHO) www.who.int/en/

References to figures and tables are in *italics*. References terms in the Glossary are followed by a 'g'.